96 GREAT INTERVIEW QUESTIONS TO ASK BEFORE YOU HIRE

PAUL FALCONE

131,192-L

amacom
American Management Association
New York • Atlanta • Boston • Chicago • Kansas City • San Francisco • Washington, D.C.
Brussels • Mexico City • Tokyo • Toronto

This publication is designed to provide accurate and authoritative information in regard to the subject matter covered. It is sold with the
understanding that the publisher is not engaged in rendering legal,
accounting, or other professional service. If legal advice or other expert
assistance is required, the services of a competent professional person
should be sought.

Library of Congress Cataloging-in-Publication Data

Falcone, Paul.
    96 great interview questions to ask before you hire / Paul
Falcone.
        p.   cm.
    ISBN 0-8144-7909-X
    1. Employment interviewing.   I. Title.
HF5549.5.I6F35   1996
    658.3'1124—dc20   96-9096
                                                       CIP

Printing number

10   9   8   7   6   5   4   3   2

Contents

To my lovely wife and best friend,
Janet,
and our two, wonderful kids—
Nina and **Sammy**—
more inspiration than any writer could hope for.

And to my dad and mom,
Carmine and **Dorothy,**
for always being there for me.

Acknowledgments

To my dear friends at AMACOM Books, especially Adrienne Hickey, Senior Acquisitions and Planning Editor, who heard my presentation at an AMA convention and envisioned the making of this book; and to Jacquie Flynn and Barbara Horowitz, AMACOM editors who worked in conjunction with Janet Frick to significantly enhance the quality of my manuscript.

To my friends and business associates who added untold value to the development of this book as it made its way through the various rounds of editing: Dick Kaumeyer, principal of the Kaumeyer Consulting Group; Dick Fearn, principal of The Human Element; Ileene Bernard, president and founder of The London Agency; Delonna Kaiser, a dear friend and a true HR pro in every sense of the word; John Favuzza, chief appraiser for Aames Financial Corporation; Larry Comp and Terry Lauter, principals of Humanomics, Inc.; Heather Hand, vice president of human resources for The City of Hope National Medical Center; Patricia Trytten, director of human resources at Executive Life Insurance Company; Sid Carp, Ph.D., organizational psychologist and fellow UCLA Extension faculty member; Kathy Shepherd, president of The Focus Agency; J. R. Cline, vice president of sales and service for Talent Tree Staffing Services; and Peter Shapiro, vice president of human resources at ElectroRent Corporation—you've all been instrumental mentors in my career.

Introduction: The Parable

Once upon a time, there was a general manager in a downtown high-rise who had final say over all new hires at her location. Although she realized how critical it was to identify and hire the best and the brightest talent for her firm, she really didn't like interviewing all that much. First, she felt fairly uncomfortable having to ask all the questions and direct the whole conversation. (Those moments of awkward silence bothered her most.) Second, she wasn't always sure of how to interpret a candidate's responses, but she felt that digging deeper was inappropriate lest she be accused of prying. Third, and most importantly, she really resented the fact that job applicants were so schooled and rehearsed in their responses. "There are just too many interviewing books and training tools available that teach people the right things to say. After a while, all their responses start sounding the same, and I don't feel like I'm actually getting to know the *real* person," she thought.

Getting past that veneer of superficial responses was detective work, and she simply didn't have the time or the inclination to invest so much of herself into the multiple rounds of interviews necessary to bring someone aboard. After all, if the candidate doesn't work out, she reasoned, there's always a ninety-day probationary window in which to "undo" the hire, right? (Wrong! It's not so easy to simply dismiss people in their ninety-day introductory periods anymore. And just because your employment application has "employment at will" verbiage doesn't necessarily get you off the hook! Wrongful termination litigation knows no time boundaries.)

Some Options . . .

As time went on and some less-than-optimal hires were made, this manager decided to improve her interviewing skills. She reasoned that making a serious investment in the art and science of career evaluations just once could have profound benefits throughout the rest of her career. Of course interviewing is a skill that needs to be honed over and over again, but if she could just build more confidence in that one area, her whole approach to building superior business teams could become stronger.

So off went the general manager to her human resources department to look into training programs, books, videos, and tapes on the topic of hiring. Wow! Was she surprised to learn of the jungle of materials available. But alas, the general manager just didn't have that much time. The tapes and videos would've been great, but finding the time to listen to tapes or watch TV was well-nigh impossible. She had also heard that many of those training books focused a lot more on theory than on practical application. After all, if she had an interview pending with a programmer analyst, a human resources manager, a secretary, or a vice-president of marketing, she needed a blueprint to successfully prepare for those specific situations.

Now, the last thing she needed was some complicated text about human resources management theory. Instead, she needed a *how*-to guide that she could turn to ten minutes before an interview to refresh her questioning skills. For only such a tool could lay out the unique interview questions for various hiring situations. She was, after all, responsible for hiring everyone from managers to professional/technical candidates to administrative support staff.

Finally, and most critically, she needed to know what to look out for in candidates' responses that might point to danger areas or issues for further investigation. Asking the questions was, as a matter of fact, only half of the equation. Knowing how to probe for more information *after* the candidate's initial response was equally if not more important in gauging the real person behind the superficial responses. That's because the farther you get away from the initial, structured query, the more you're called upon to employ your interpretative and evaluative decision-making skills. Therefore, she needed to know:

- What might trip off danger signals in a candidate's response to a particular question?
- What kinds of superficial responses deserve more in-depth probing?
- How could she find a way of matching the candidate's personal style to her company's corporate culture?

The Solution

96 Great Interview Questions to Ask Before *You Hire* is a practical, how-to guide for any hiring situation. This book teaches you how to evaluate:

- What is the individual's motivation for changing jobs?
- Could your organization fill the person's needs?
- Is this individual committed to progressive career management, or is he "recruiter's bait" waiting to jump at the next offer?
- Worse, could your interview merely be a ploy to leverage more money at his current company by accepting a counteroffer?
- Does this person adhere strictly to her job duties, or does she constantly assume responsibilities beyond her written job description and attempt to reinvent her job in light of her company's changing needs?
- How well does this candidate distinguish between high- and low-payoff activities, how does he handle stress, how does he accept constructive criticism, and what kind of work ethic does he have?

The Pièce de Résistance

96 Great Interview Questions to Ask Before *You Hire* assumes that there are two levels of interviewing that are critical before you make a hiring decision: First, you interview the candidate who weaves a tale of past performance and achievements. That historical perspective helps you project what the future will look like because past behaviors will most likely be repeated. Second, you interview the candidate's former immediate supervisors, who can verify your insights into the individual's ability to excel in your company! For only with an objective, third-party evaluation can you be sure that candidates' historical recounting of their performance is accurate.

More significantly, third-party references are one of the most valid tools available for predicting the future. Guaranteed? No. But insightful as to what it's like working side by side with this person every day? Absolutely! Discerning as to where the person will need the most support in the first 90 days? Of course! Incisive in terms of how best to manage the person either by providing lots of structure, direction, and feedback or by allowing him to be an independent, solo flyer with lots of autonomy and independent decision-making authority? You betcha! And while we're at it, we'll develop a methodology for getting former employers to open up to you over the phone and share their feelings about a particular candidate's abilities to make a successful transition into your company.

So let's get ready to put together an interviewing and reference-checking blueprint that will catapult your candidate evaluation skills to new heights, increase your confidence in mastering every hiring situation, and help you build better teams of coworkers who will give your organization the competitive advantage.

Best Practices in Recruitment and Selection

This book is a complete, hands-on guide to the employment process. There's not much theory to wade through—just questions to add immediate critical mass to your interview and suggestions for interpreting the answers you get. Written for senior managers, first-line supervisors, contingency recruiters, and human resources professionals, it guides you from start to finish through the entire employment process by highlighting:

- Questions to ask candidates through multiple rounds of interviews
- Reference-checking queries to validate your insights into the person's ability to excel in your company
- Counteroffer preparation
- Job offer negotiations

The premise for this book is a simple one: The best workers have the most options. Positioning yourself and your company to identify individuals with the strongest track records and to appeal to those top performers is what the interviewing and selection process is all about. You are both buyer and seller, critical observer and attractive commodity. For nothing less than your organization's bottom line is at stake.

Legal Compliance. The primary caveat, however, is to keep your questioning patterns within legal boundaries so that you don't unnecessarily expose your company. Lost wages litigation, wrongful failure to hire, and other legal remedies exist for workers who have had their rights violated. Consequently, the queries and questioning techniques that follow will not only provide you with refreshing insights into candidates' behaviors, but you can rest assured that they will also keep you from running afoul of the law. Just to be safe, refer now to Chapter 18: Staying Within the Law: Questions to Avoid to During the Interview. It will provide you with the ten most common errors to look out for.

Behavioral Interview Questions. In addition, the most successful technique for adding dimension to superficial answers lies in employing a behavioral interview questioning format. Behavioral interviewing techniques attempt to relate a candidate's answers to specific past experiences and focus on projecting potential performance from past actions. By relating a candidate's answers to specific past experiences, you'll develop much more reliable indicators of how the individual will most likely act in the future. Behavioral questions do not deny that people can learn from their mistakes and alter their behaviors. They do, however, assume that a person's future behavior will closely reflect past actions.

Behavioral interview questions call for on-the-spot self-analysis. There are two main types of behavioral formats: self-appraisal and situational questions. *Self-appraisal* queries ask a candidate, "What is it about you that makes you feel a certain way or want to do something?" For example, "What is it about you that makes you get totally involved in your work to a point where you lose track of the time?" Similarly, the self-appraisal format may ask for a third-party validation of your actions: "What would your supervisor say about that?"

Other examples of self-appraisal queries include:

"On a scale of 1 to 10 (1 meaning that you're lenient and understanding, 10 meaning that you're demanding and critical), how do you see yourself as a supervisor? Why?"

"If you had the choice of working in a marketing or a finance environment, which would you choose and why?"

"In the future, how do you think you would handle an employee termination in those same circumstances?"

Situational queries, like self-appraisal queries, look for concrete experience as an indicator of future behavior. The standard behavioral interviewing query begins with the paradigm, "Tell me about a time when you took action without getting your boss's prior approval," "Describe the last time you assumed responsibility for a task that was clearly outside of your job description," or "Give me an example of a time when you had to make a critical decision in your boss's absence." Notice the specific linkage to concrete past experiences and situations.

The beauty of this questioning methodology is that it can be applied to anything: a candidate's greatest strengths and weaknesses, his supervisory and sales styles, his communication skills, or the last time he fired someone. As a result, behavioral questions ensure spontaneity since candidates can't prepare for them in advance. Rehearsed answers to traditional queries go by the wayside in this ad hoc interviewing environment where candidates tell stories about their real-life performance. And because they tie responses to concrete past actions, they minimize the candidate's inclination to exaggerate answers. Hence, you're assured of more accurate answers in the selection process, and you're provided with specific ammunition to use later down the line in the reference-checking process.

Figure I-1 is a wishbone diagram showing the unpredictable course of a behavioral interviewing question. Watch where the behavioral interview questions lead this conversation. Because this technique is critical to advanced candidate evaluations, we'll employ it throughout the rest of the book.

How Is This Book Structured?

96 Great Interview Questions to Ask Before *You Hire* is divided into twenty-one chapters. Parts I and II, the first seventeen chapters, contain a total

Figure I-1. The unpredictable course of behavioral interview questioning.

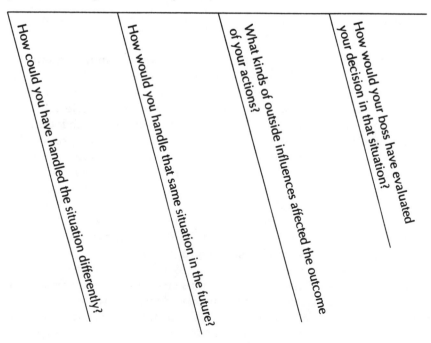

"**Tell me about a time when you** . . . felt it important to take it upon yourself to bring bad news to your boss."

How could you have handled the situation differently?

How would you handle that same situation in the future?

What kinds of outside influences affected the outcome of your actions?

How would your boss have evaluated your decision in that situation?

of ninety-six questions, approximately five questions per chapter. Each chapter either addresses individual characteristics (for identifying a candidate's career stability or promotions through the ranks, for example) or highlights functional interviewing strategies (for evaluating secretaries, senior managers, salespeople, or professional/technical staff).

Although every attempt has been made to include the most practical queries for a specific hiring need, no topic is all-inclusive. For example, although there are ten primary questions to ask sales candidates, there are other areas of the book that will complement those five key questions. You might logically pull information out of the chapters on career stability, achievement-anchored questions, or likability and compatibility to round out your sales interview. Similarly, you could employ traditional queries with holistic interviewing questions when evaluating professional/technical candidates like accountants, programmers, or paralegals. The point is, it's up to you to mix and match the questioning techniques as you see fit. One thing's for sure, though: Talent doesn't exist in a vacuum and has to be benchmarked to your style of doing business. Consequently, you'll have plenty of latitude to customize the information for your particular interviewing situation!

You'll note as well that many of the questions are two-pronged queries that require the candidate to make logical connections and provide greater background depth in response. Those connectors not only measure how well the individual breaks down information into its component parts, but they force the candidate to tie together all the loose ends when concluding. Two-pronged questions are also beneficial because they allow you, the interviewer, to be more specific in your queries. The old "one-liners" don't go far enough nowadays in gathering the in-depth data necessary to make a hiring calculation. By stating your questions more specifically and intimating how you want the candidate to interpret your query, you'll automatically increase your control of the hiring situation.

High-Performance Questioning Techniques for a Competitive Business Environment

The "Why Ask This Question?" section after each query attempts to crystallize why the question is indeed valid. It addresses what you are attempting to measure in a candidate's response. It also specifies the ideal circumstances for employing the question in sales, secretarial, professional/technical, or senior management interviews.

The "Analyzing the Response" section after the query is typically much longer because it attempts to highlight:

- What you should expect to hear in a typical candidate's response
- What variations on this questioning theme exist to perhaps re-phrase the query in a slightly different manner
- What danger signs you should look out for in evaluating candidate responses
- How you could employ behavioral interviewing techniques to add concrete, historical dimensions to the individual's response and thereby avoid canned and rehearsed answers
- How you could look for contrary evidence that further challenges candidates to develop or defend their answers
- How you would subsequently verify a candidate's responses via a reference check

A key advantage to this book therefore lies not only in the "cataloging" of high-yield questions for various hiring situations but also in the quick and insightful interpretations of expected responses. After all, once you're forewarned about the hot buttons and danger zones that could spell subpar performance or an unacceptable work ethic, you'll be better equipped to avoid marginal hires. And since no human being is perfect, you will be in a better position for damage control if you understand each candidate's shortcomings. You will gain these critical insights both through information that the candidate volunteers during your interview and through external verifications (reference checks from past employers).

Finally, Part III (Chapters 18 through 21) provides practical information in terms of getting the most for your recruitment dollar while minimizing your legal exposure. Chapter 19, "Telephone Screening Interviews: Formats and Follow-Ups for Swift Information Gathering" takes a practical look at phone assessments in order to determine whether a candidate is qualified for an in-person meeting. Such screening interviews are exceptionally effective at guarding your time since a ten minute up-front investment could potentially save hours of your (and a candidate's) time. Employ the matrix in this section to quickly and efficiently determine a candidate's viability!

Chapter 21, "Maximizing Your Recruitment Resources," will provide a cost-benefit analysis for choosing contingency recruitment versus retained search firms. It will also address the critical role that research firms provide in "unbundling" the search process. Finally, it will highlight one of the best-kept secrets in town for locating high-probability candidates for free—your local outplacement firm's job development department.

So pick up a pencil and a highlighter and join me for a behind-the-scenes look at sophisticated candidate evaluation techniques that will maximize all your recruitment and selection efforts!

Bear in mind, however, that this book is not intended as a legal guide for the complex issues surrounding candidate selection, reference checking, and other aspects of hiring and employment practices. Because the book does not purport to render legal advice, it should not be used in place of an attorney when proper legal counsel and guidance become necessary.

PART I

Interview Questions to Identify High-Performance Candidates

One

For Openers: Five Traditional Interview Questions and Their Interpretations

Let's begin by examining the most often used interview questions and putting a new spin on their interpretations. These questions have stood the test of time, and we should consequently recognize their value in the candidate assessment process. Their inherent weakness, of course, lies in their overuse: Most of us can remember being asked these very questions during our own past interviews. And job-finding books and career magazines abound with suggested responses to help candidates "steer clear of the interview questioning snare" vis-à-vis these popular queries waiting to trip them up.

Our exercise in this first topic, however, isn't to employ questions just because they've been around for a long time. And it's certainly not to offer candidates an opportunity to practice their well-rehearsed lines! We will, instead, offer new interpretations in reading candidate responses.

1. Tell me about your greatest strength. What's the greatest asset you'll bring to our company?

Why Ask This Question?

The "greatest strength" question works well as an icebreaker because most people are fairly comfortable talking about what makes them special and what they like. Every job candidate is ready for this one because it gets so much attention in the career press. Job candidates are also aware that this query is used as a lead-in to a natural follow-up question (which

3

is much tougher to answer): "What's your greatest weakness?" Still, the "greatest strength" question isn't a throwaway because it can reveal a lot about an individual's self-perception. So let's open it up for a moment.

Analyzing the Response

There are two issues to watch out for in measuring candidates' responses: First, candidates often give lofty answers with lists of adjectives that they think you want to hear and that actually add very little value to your meeting. Second, candidates' strengths may fail to match your unit's needs, and as such could weigh as a negative swing factor in the selection process.

RED FLAGS. Watch out for people who give long inventories of "fluff adjectives" regarding their nobler traits, such as *hard-working, intelligent, loyal,* and *committed*. Adjectives are nothing but unproven claims. They waste time and delay getting to what you really want to get out of this meeting: concrete proof of how the individual will fit in and contribute to the team. Consequently, you'll have to keep the candidate on track by following up on these adjective lists with requests for practical applications. For example, when a candidate says that she's proudest of the fact that she's a hard worker, you might respond:

"Hard workers are always good to find. Give me an example of how hard you work relative to your peers."

or

"Hard work usually results in above-average results. How has your hard work paid off in terms of the quantity of your output or the quality of your work product?"

or

"Hard work in our company boils down to working late hours fairly often and occasionally coming in on Saturdays. How does your present company define hard work?"

or

"How has your boss recognized your hard work? How would she say that you could have worked smarter, not harder?"

The idea here is to *qualify* this person's generic response. The second red flag issue occurs when a candidate's strengths fail to match your organizational needs. For example, a candidate may respond, "I guess I would say that I'm proudest of my progression through the ranks with my last company. I was promoted four times in as many years, and I feel that a company's ultimate reward to its people can be found in the recognition it gives via promotions and ongoing training." That's an excellent response. The position you're filling, however, may offer very few vertical growth opportunities because you need someone who would be satisfied with very repetitive work. This is a classic case of "Right person—wrong opportunity," and the "greatest strength" query will have done its job of identifying a candidate's motives and expectations. Consequently, you might opt to disqualify the candidate for this particular position.

2. What's your greatest weakness?

Why Ask This Question?

Other variations on this theme include:

"What would you consider to be your occasional fault or 'over-strength'?"

"Of your past supervisors, who would give you the weakest reference and why?"

"What one area do you really need to work on in your career to become more effective on a day-to-day basis?"

You would think that most job candidates have preplanned responses to these often-asked queries. That's not, however, always the case. There are still a surprising number of people out there who give very little advance thought to this common self-evaluation query. You could use that element of surprise to your advantage.

Analyzing the Response

The "greatest weakness" question is somewhat unnerving because it causes discomfort. After all, no one wants to discuss shortcomings. Although the purpose of the question is certainly not to make anyone uncomfortable, many unsuspecting individuals will use this entree as an invitation to "come clean" and bare their souls to you. That's when you'll learn that they sometimes run late getting to work, feel intimidated in any kind of public speaking forum, or tend to be too overbearing with coworkers.

RED FLAGS. Note as well that it's a poor answer for candidates to respond that they have no weaknesses. After all, interviewing, to a large extent, is a game to see how deftly a person lands on her feet. By admitting no weaknesses, the person refuses to "play the game," so to speak. In that case, you'll need to provide a gentle nudging along the lines of, "Oh, Janet, everyone has some kind of weakness. What should I expect to be your shortcomings if we work together on a day-to-day basis?" If that coaxing fails to produce a response, beware the precedent that is being set toward poor communications and lack of openness.

Good Answers. In contrast, what are acceptable responses that place a candidate in a favorable light? Look for replies that center around the person's impatience with her own performance, inclination toward being a perfectionist (which could slow the individual down, but guarantees quality results), or tendency to avoid delegating work to others for fear that it won't get done to the candidate's high expectations. In short, the wisest "weaknesses" are strengths taken to a fault. After all, people who are impatient with their own performance typically have very high expectations of themselves. Neatniks can't bear the possibility of sending out letters that contain errors. And those who have difficulty delegating are results-oriented, focused individuals who generally don't watch the clock.

How to Get More Mileage Out of the Question. Once again, the key to adding a broader dimension to the candidate's response lies in employing a behavioral interviewing format. Try looking for *contrary evidence* that focuses on the negative impact of the person's actions. For example, typical comebacks you could use to the reply "I have problems delegating work to other people because I find that the end result doesn't meet my expectations" might include:

- *Tell me about the last time* you didn't delegate work to a subordinate and you were left handling a disproportionate amount of the workload. How did you feel about that? How did you handle that situation differently the next time?
- *Give me an example of a time when* your not having delegated work

to a direct report left that person feeling that his career development needs weren't being met.

- *Share with me a circumstance in which* you were frustrated by your boss's inability to delegate work to you. How did you eventually gain that person's trust?

The variations are limitless. Candidates have no way of preparing "canned" responses to your interview questions, and therein lies the true beauty of the behavioral query.

3. What was your favorite position, and what role did your boss play in making it so unique?

Why Ask This Question?

Much like the "greatest strength" question, this query invites the interviewee to reflect on positive and comfortable emotions. It also prepares the stage for the related question to follow (which is much harder to address), "What was your least favorite position or company?" Still, there are telling clues in the individual's response, so let's look for the salient issues.

Analyzing the Response

Human resources professionals and executive recruiters will attest to how warm and cozy this query generally makes candidates feel. Candidates' body language often will totally relax, and warm smiles will appear. Their responses, however, could indeed knock them out of consideration for a job when they sell a love for a particular aspect of a past position that you are not offering.

RED FLAGS. Take the case of a marketing representative named Joan. When the question about favorite jobs came her way, she mistakenly mentioned a past job that was extremely creative and got her out of the office a few hours a week. She had worked for an international firm that offered the opportunity to entertain foreign dignitaries, and she had been responsible for giving tours of the company's solar energy plant.

Granted, that may be why that particular job stood out in Joan's memory. However, because the job she was applying for didn't offer those nontraditional perks, she ended up selling her love of tasks that she wouldn't be handling on the new job. She consequently weakened her case because the company felt that she was overqualified—in other words, the organization couldn't offer her the glamour and variety she was accustomed to and felt she wouldn't be stimulated in its nine-to-five environment.

Note as well that statistically a majority of people leave their jobs because of personality conflicts with their boss. No matter how well the company fares, once that key interpersonal relationship sours, there's very little opportunity left for a subordinate to assume greater responsibilities, earn significantly more money, or remain part of the unit's succession plan. Hence, you want to connect what role a boss played in making a job a favorite position, just as you want to tie in the supervisor's role in making a job a least favorite position.

4. What was your least favorite position? What role did your boss play in your career at that point?

Why Ask This Question?

The body language changes very quickly when candidates are presented with an invitation to criticize or censure a former boss or company. After all, this query baits individuals to complain about the people to whom they should be most loyal. The ideal candidate response avoids subjective, personal interpretations that force respondents to defend their past actions. Instead, a solid response will address objective issues that place an impersonal distance between the candidate and the external factors that interfered with his reaching his personal best. In short, look for job candidates' abilities to objectively evaluate a situation rather than irrationally react to it.

Analyzing the Response

RED FLAGS. Little need be said regarding candidates who shoot down past bosses. These people automatically place themselves in a victim posture by assigning blame to others. They also show little interviewing sophistication because they fail to realize that you are taking their answers with a grain of salt: After all, most managers can relate to being the brunt of a subordinate's criticism. Why, therefore, should the candidate expect you to choose sides when he is describing only one side of a complaint? Besides, the candidate's former boss isn't even there to present her side of the story, so why should you be forced to show empathy to one party and not the other? No doubt about it—talking poorly about a past employer is one of the worst things candidates can do in the interviewing process.

Good Answers. In discussing a least favorite position and the boss's role in making it so, candidates will usually address the interpersonal challenges they had with bosses who stifled their career growth. Here's how certain positive responses might sound:

> "What I disliked most about my former company is the fact that it offered very little risk and reward. It was a very mature company with exceptionally long staff tenure. I respect any company that can build loyalty and longevity in the ranks, but my boss, the CEO, was preparing to retire, and we senior managers were not expected to 'step outside of the box,' so to speak, when it came to taking risks. That wasn't the type of corporate culture that I wanted."

or

> "My least favorite position is unfortunately the position I now hold. My boss, the chief operating officer, inadequately prepared for a change in the business environment. The firm made hay while the sun was shining when interest rates were their lowest in thirty years. However, he put all the company's eggs in the refinance basket and developed few contingency plans for the inevitable increase in rates. That kind of 'quarterly profit' mentality went against my better business judgment."

or

> "If I had to critique a past employer's performance, I would have to say that working for Jay Panico, the senior vice president of sales at XYZ Company, had the most challenges. We worked very well together personally, but Jay needed to be much more proactive in terms of anticipating the workload. He prided himself on putting out fires. My style, conversely, was to forecast potential problems before they arose. It got very tiring after a while and took the fun out of coming to work every day."

or

"My least favorite boss was probably Denise Spaulding because she was so cynical. She provided our team of first-line supervisors with little structure and direction in our day. Her door was closed most of the time, and she was openly uncomfortable hearing about our problem issues and concerns. That made relying on her as a resource fairly impractical. Worst of all, she spoke poorly about the firm often and was renowned for causing an overactive grapevine."

These solid responses share objective evaluations that place no blame on anyone while gently probing realistic organizational or individual weaknesses.

5. Where do you see yourself in five years?

Why Ask This Question?

This question is a known showstopper because it triggers a candidate's "wishful response" mechanism. You'll hear about people who want to be retired on a desert isle. You'll see flower stand owners in the making. Those who want your job five years from now might even make you a little nervous! And what about those respondents who say that five years from now they want to be holding the same job they're applying for today? So much for healthy career ambition!

If it seems as if anything and everything candidates say will weigh against them, you're realizing the pitfalls of this question. The fact that candidates simply seem to throw caution to the wind might provide some interesting insights that might not otherwise surface during your meeting. After all, if the candidate's five-year goals have absolutely nothing to do with the job you're offering, how could you build long-term plans around the person?

Analyzing the Response

First of all, when candidates respond with a far-out answer like retiring to Tahiti or opening a bowling alley, note down their responses. Then bring them back to reality by requesting that they tie their responses in to the business world and your industry. Second, when candidates name a title other than the one they are applying for (i.e. speaking prematurely about promotional opportunities), question: "How long would you expect to have to work in our company to realize that goal? What skills and experiences would you have to master in order to make that five-year dream a reality?"

Good Answers. A realistic response will typically show that a candidate's long-term goal will only be attainable after three or four years. Getting the prospective new hire to commit to that number of years sets up your long-term expectations and minimizes the chances of premature turnover due to "lack of sufficient growth opportunities." It's not uncommon, after all, to see new hires leave a company after six short months and decry the lack of promotional opportunities at the firm.

In addition, a smart response will avoid naming job titles other than the position the candidate is applying for. The proper candidate response will, instead, place more emphasis on the assumption of broadened responsibilities at the current position. So instead of listening to a staff accountant address her desire to attain her first divisional controllership with your Fortune 500 organization, you'll hear more about the candidate's desire to assume broader duties as a staff accountant that allow her to make a positive impact on your department:

> "Ms. Employer, I believe I can make the greatest contribution to your company by focusing on my general staff accounting skills. That's where my total focus lies. Where it leads me in five years, I hope you'll eventually tell me. But I want you to know that I'll be open to adding value to your organization in whatever way you see fit."

Voilà—a balanced, logical, and realistic self-assessment that addresses your organization's needs and that person's ability to provide solutions to those needs.

Two

Achievement-Anchored Questions: Measuring Individuals' Awareness of Their Accomplishments

No issue is more telling in the candidate selection process than measuring individuals' assessments of their own achievements. Not all people in the career change process will suddenly develop newfound insights into their individual accomplishments and ability to affect a future employer's bottom line. Still, any candidates mounting a realistic job search campaign in today's survival-of-the-fittest workplace should realize that corporate executives are taking a harder, more judgmental line on new hires. Therefore, the "career introspection" that ideally belongs at the onset of all candidates' job search campaigns should mandate that all interviewees create a personalized mission statement to identify what, how, and where they can bring about change in a future organization.

That being said, reality bears out a different truth. Fewer than 25 percent of candidates will be able to articulate clearly what distinguishes them from their peers.

6. What makes you stand out among your peers?

Why Ask This Question?

At first glance, such a simple query appears to offer only a modest challenge to the average candidate preparing for job change. However, the simplicity of the question doesn't necessarily equate with the difficulty and demand it places on the candidate struggling to identify a response. Although that response can take a myriad of forms—increased revenues, decreased operational costs, streamlined work flow, or creative achievements—most job applicants give scant thought to the value they've brought to past companies. It's exactly that "work for a paycheck" entitlement mentality that you want to avoid in your quest for high-performance, high-velocity career candidates.

Beginning with the premise that only 25 percent of the working population will be able to articulate its uniqueness as "corporate assets," you'll begin your selection interview with a tool to identify proven performers with healthy levels of self-esteem. Bear in mind that not every opening in your organization will necessitate a high level of self-confidence. Still, when it comes to winnowing the chaff from the wheat for higher-profile positions, this query is the sine qua non of all final hiring decisions.

Analyzing the Response

This simple litmus test that measures self-esteem will generate a myriad of answers from "I have no idea—I just sit in a room with other staff accountants crunching out numbers all day" to "I took it upon myself to reconfigure our existing software systems to increase our customer satisfaction index by 32 percent." The latter response obviously begs for clarification: "What motivated you to rethink your existing way of doing business? How did you involve your department and get it to buy in to your idea? How did you come up with that 32 percent figure?" and so on. But it sure is refreshing to find candidates prepared to articulate the particular nature of their achievements.

RED FLAGS. The former response, though, is problematic. You shouldn't necessarily expect bells and whistles in a candidate's retort. After all, the majority of people most likely won't have single-handedly saved their organization from financial ruin or earned it a spot on *Forbes Magazine's* list of the best companies in America. You should, however, expect the candidate to accept your invitation to respond to this challenging question. A response like, "I don't know—I've never thought about it before" refuses your invitation to engage in the conversation. It's fine if the person never thought about it before, but now's the time for him to articulate a response!

So if the candidate backs off from you this early in the interview process, it sets a tone for the rest of the meeting: You may have to extract answers from this person like pulling teeth. That precedent impedes open and insightful communications focusing on how the individual is ready to make a contribution to your organization. If you're able to find that out five minutes into your interview, you'll have saved yourself lots of time and energy.

Good Answers. Candidate responses could be as simple as:

"I'm totally dedicated to my work and define myself by the great job that I do."

or

"I have a track record for assuming responsibilities above and beyond the call of duty, and I'm always willing to go the extra mile to get the job done."

or

"I'm proudest of the fact that I was hired to grow a region of ten sales offices within a year and successfully met my target goals by the end of the third quarter."

These kinds of comebacks reveal focus and direction. A sense of strength and determination arises merely from the candidate's accepting the challenge of responding to this daunting question. You should applaud those who don't flinch in coming up with an on-the-spot answer, no matter how simple or even awkward it sounds. Bear in mind that right and wrong answers have no say in this particular questioning scenario. What's critical is the timing of the response and the conviction with which it's stated. You'll have plenty of opportunities throughout the rest of interview to gauge factual information. Your measuring rod here focuses on eye contact, posture, and confidence; the candidate either backs off from your challenge or rises to the occasion.

7. What have you done on your present/last position to increase your organization's top-line revenues?

Why Ask This Question?

At first glance, it appears that this query belongs in the section of this book dedicated to sales professionals. And you may very well want to employ this question in dealing with line candidates who have a direct impact on your company's bottom-line profits. The reason why this query occurs here, however, is that any member of an organization—line or staff—is capable of generating revenues for a company. It may not be in the traditional sales sense, but it makes money nonetheless.

Analyzing the Response

Good Answers. A secretary, for example, may come up with the idea of adding a response mechanism to the back of a fund-raising letter so that donations could be returned immediately (rather than waiting for a fund-raiser to follow up with a phone call). A corporate travel coordinator might find that he's able to offer travel services to another company, thereby earning small commissions that can offset expenses in your travel budget. Or a training director might see a valuable market for her training programs outside of her company and generate add-on business revenues by offering on-site training workshops to other companies in the field. However you look at it, these nonsales employees have made money for their past employers and will probably bring similar creative insights to your firm.

What happens if nonsales candidates are unable to come up with an answer to this challenging query? Then use an alternative query that will help them identify how they've benefited a previous company from a cost-savings standpoint.

8. What have you done to reduce your department's operational costs or to save time?

Why Ask This Question?

Staff employees typically identify their achievements via their ability to reduce operational expenses (as opposed to generating revenues). Staff departments like human resources, accounting, office services, and information technology are noncore segments of a business that support the revenue-raising activities of line departments. Staff workers therefore focus on increasing the efficiency of the organization by building a stronger infrastructure to get things done. The more efficient the systems to bring product to market, the more time is saved. As the saying goes, time is money. So asking a support or staff worker to identify decreased costs or saved time provides the candidate with a comfortable alternative if the question about generating revenue fails.

Analyzing the Response

This question is critical if your goal is to identify "economic advocates" who view your company as if it were their own. Economic advocacy theory proposes that employers totally involve their workers in the costs of running business operations and the revenues and profits currently being generated. Companies that espouse this theory practice a policy of "open financials" to empower workers with the necessary information to conduct the business as if it were their own. After all, sharing the monthly costs of office space, supplies, and parking passes with employees goes a long way in developing a sense of appreciation for the costs of doing business. Likewise, sharing revenue goals builds camaraderie among informed and empowered workers.

Regardless of whether (or to what degree) your particular company espouses such financial disclosure practices, finding people who look beyond their immediate functional areas to reduce costs will have a direct impact on your bottom line. Committed employees generate ideas to increase the work flow and suggest improvements outside of their departments. Such a profit-and-loss orientation should prove a significant benefit to any company wanting to redefine itself in a quickly changing marketplace.

Good Answers. A human resources manager might reduce annual cost-per-hire expenses (hiring costs divided by the number of new hires) by implementing a successful employee referral program. A production control coordinator might increase unit output by eliminating minor costs associated with rework. Or a fax attendant might have taken it upon himself to employ Post-It flyers instead of cover letters, thereby saving one facsimile page per document.

How to get more mileage out of the question. If candidates have a difficult time coming up with ways to prove their "economic advocacy" tendencies, take them through a mini-questioning scenario that helps them mentally move from the features of their jobs (what they merely do to earn a paycheck) to the benefits they provide their employers. Let's look at three separate candidates to see how you could encourage candidates to attain a higher realization of their achievements:

Step 1: I assume, Mary, that as a fax attendant/plant engineer/controller, your job is to coordinate a large workload and meet very specific deadlines for your department. How do you measure your productivity?

Initial Responses

Fax attendant: "By the number of faxes I send out and receive."

Plant engineer: "By the quality of the repairs I make so that problems, once fixed, don't interrupt production again."

Controller: "By output of my payables, receivables, and payroll staff."

Step 2: And how does your company, in a broader sense, benefit from your achievements?

Enhanced Responses

Fax attendant: "I facilitate communications and get the proper information into the hands of decision makers so that business gets carried out."

Plant engineer: "I support the manufacturing production process by calibrating test instruments to ensure that the liquids and powders flowing through the production cylinders are distributed equally."

Controller: "I ensure that payroll is met each pay period and maintain the integrity of our credit rating."

Step 3: Then I would ask you to go even beyond that in terms of your ultimate impact on the company's bottom line. How have your activities reduced your company's operating expenses or saved time by increasing the work flow?

Ultimate Responses

Fax attendant: "I've been able to juggle a higher volume of inbound and outbound faxes without error, so I've cut down on unnecessary phone calls, increased our department's monthly production numbers, and made my boss's life a lot easier."

Plant engineer: "The calibration mechanisms in the testing instruments that we used to measure powder and liquid distribution were refined to increase efficiencies. Those increases in efficiency measures helped the company control the production process and reduce costs associated with inaccurate container injection."

Controller: "I've been able to keep the financial end of my company running smoothly. I never missed a payroll deadline, I increased the effectiveness of our accounts receivable program by training my people to become actively involved collectors, and I ensured that our creditworthiness was untainted."

Voilà—a simple three-step questioning method to help uncover candidates' achievements by questioning them on a benefit-to-solution level as opposed to a more traditional evaluation that focuses strictly on the features of their respective jobs.

9. What has been your most creative achievement at work?

Why Ask This Question?

Creativity in this case has nothing to do with "artsy" stuff or candidates' needs for aesthetic satisfaction at work. Instead, it centers around coming up with unique solutions to existing challenges that face companies every day. Individuals with penchants for reframing problems and customizing solutions deserve a special place in your organization. The question is, How do you make people feel comfortable discussing their discoveries when cultural and personal barriers get in the way? After all, lots of candidates will equate discussing their achievements with bragging about themselves.

Analyzing the Response

How to Get More Mileage Out of the Question. A prudent way to get candidates to open up to you regarding the creative solutions they've offered their past employers is to apply a technique from the behavioral psychology realm called "appropriate sharing." Appropriate sharing is a therapeutic technique to overcome "blocking" tendencies where respondents have difficulty answering questions that make them personally or culturally uncomfortable. The premise of the technique lies in sharing personal anecdotes that show the candidate that you've been there too. Once that mutual level of understanding is established, candidates will hopefully feel more at ease exchanging personal information about themselves.

Here's an example of an introduction into this sharing technique: "Marlene, one of the things we value most in our company is people who look at problems more creatively and try to find solutions to issues that impede our growth. When I originally interviewed here, the employer asked me how creatively I solved problems at work. Well, I didn't quite understand what she meant until after the interview was over. And then I kicked myself for not being able to give her an answer on the spot. But

I'd like you to think about one problem—no matter how minor it might seem—that slowed down your department or created extra work with very little payoff. Then tell me what you did to make the situation better. Or even if you did nothing, tell me what you possibly could have done to change the situation. . . ."

Obviously there's no need to go overboard in creating a comfortable environment to encourage open responses. After all, you don't want to coddle the candidate. Still, painting a picture of how you responded to the question—for example, how you ordered Post-It notes to replace fax cover sheets—when it was asked of you during a past interview should allay a shy candidate's fears about revealing creative achievements that maximized the work flow.

Unfortunately, many candidates don't even realize the positive impact of their actions. Although your role in the interview process certainly isn't to build strangers' self-esteem, it's certainly exciting to watch the lights go on as candidates play out their past achievements before your very eyes. Swapping tales about creative achievements might be an excellent place to start when dealing with self-effacing individuals.

10. What would your current supervisors say makes you most valuable to them?

Why Ask This Question?

Your final query in this section should focus on mapping out the direct benefits of candidates' actions. In the preceding examples, you've probed individuals' impact on the company or department via increased revenues, decreased operating expenses, or time saved. An alternative lies in questioning interviewees' impact on their bosses. Although senior managerial and professional/technical candidates will typically be able to affect an organization's bottom line via the breath and scope of their responsibilities, lower-level employees might feel intimidated at having to address such grand and global issues. Provide them an alternative by setting their sights on a much more definable and concrete result— namely, making their bosses' lives easier.

Analyzing the Response

How are bosses' lives made easier? Well, for the typical administrative support or light industrial worker, aiming to please a supervisor could very well define the individual's overriding career philosophy. After all, junior-level employees typically don't see their contributions recognized in the monthly newsletter or on the company's 10Q statement. Still, having relieved the boss of time-consuming tasks or having electronically organized a former paper trail system might have been the primary accolade on the candidate's last performance appraisal.

How to Get More Mileage Out of the Question. As a matter of fact, the key to generating a realistic response centers around the performance evaluation process. If a candidate has difficulty articulating how her boss's job was made easier, then question what the boss focused on during the last performance review. Namely, the sections entitled "Strengths" and "Areas for Development" target tasks that the individual already performs particularly well or should focus on developing to an even greater degree. Similarly, question tasks in which the individual is expected to train coworkers. If an employee assumes quasi-supervisory responsibilities even for very limited projects, that's usually enough to lighten the supervisor's workload.

Three

Holistic Interview Queries: Challenging Candidates to Assess Themselves

Holistic questions assess how individuals see themselves fitting into your corporate team. Holistic queries attempt to measure the whole person—the candidate's work patterns, career goals, and ability to see the global impact of his actions. They are usually very broad, open-ended queries that candidates find challenging to answer on the spot because of their all-encompassing nature. However, they successfully measure people's broad perceptions of their self-worth, self-esteem, and potential abilities to contribute.

Holistic questions aim to surface candidates' self-admitted short-comings, their interest in the technical and analytical aspects of their occupational specialties, their capacity for self-critical insight, and their inclination to distribute time and energy in proportion to the payoff potential of a given task. Moreover, beyond engaging candidates in assessing their overall job responsibilities, these questions will also help you more clearly define your needs when attempting to fill a newly created position.

For example, let's say you're creating a new position for a programmer analyst to aid in the transition from your in-house loan servicing program to an off-the-shelf software application. You know what you want to achieve in creating this new position, but you're not exactly sure what "pedigree" or background orientation you'll need in the ideal candidate. You may want someone who understands the pressures and protocol inherent to the data conversion process. Maybe you need someone with a strong background in artificial intelligence, or perhaps an individual with an exceptionally strong understanding of mortgage banking processes (making the position a hybrid of programmer analyst and business analyst).

Whatever your emphasis, it's clear that not all programmer analysts will possess the desired orientation. People out of mortgage banking may lack the requisite artificial intelligence orientation. Candidates who are currently working in your target application may know nothing of the mortgage loan process. And individuals who have successfully mastered conversions from a more strategic vantage point may lack the desired hands-on programming and coding background that will ultimately make this transitional project a success.

More than anything else, therefore, holistic queries help you define how candidates sees themselves and their brand of programming and analysis. Armed with the individual's self-evaluation, you'll be better positioned to select the most appropriate orientations, experience histories, and skill sets in the candidate selection process. Following are some of the more popular applications of holistic interviewing techniques. See which ones apply to your immediate needs most.

11. What are the broad responsibilities of a [*job title*]?

Why Ask This Question?

Defining broad responsibilities is somewhat cumbersome, but it should challenge a candidate to do some out-loud brainstorming that helps differentiate and order primary and secondary job responsibilities. It will dovetail nicely into amplifying the person's resumé highlights, and it will also paint a picture for you of the person's comfort zones. (Those areas will typically surface first in the response.) See whether the candidate's feedback matches the critical elements that encompass your opening, and probe for details regarding areas that the candidate initially overlooks in her response.

Analyzing the Response

One very common mistake made by employers today is to list an opening for a secretary with an employment agency and then provide very little critical detail regarding the desired candidate's work habits, primary duties, and track record of achievements. "A secretary is a secretary is a secretary" goes this flawed line of thinking, and few examples provide better insight into the usefulness of this interviewing question.

Watch how various candidates will paint much different pictures of their jobs in response to your query regarding their broad responsibilities:

Candidate 1: The broad responsibilities of a secretary include lowering the company's operational costs by saving time, representing the company in her boss's absence, and making decisions that further the company's interests. I've achieved these goals, Ms. Employer, by putting together correspondence with pinpoint grammatical and contextual accuracy, by screening phone calls with a true customer service attitude, and by doing everything else necessary in a business office to keep my boss one step ahead of the game. I totally automated her agenda using a personal information manager. I also set up all of my departmental work logs on a shareware software so that my boss could spot-check where I was on any specific project without leaving her desk. In short, I see the secretarial role as quasi-administrative, quasi-personal, quasi-technical, and quasi-managerial.

Candidate 2: The broad responsibilities of a secretary center around being one step ahead of all your projects so that your boss can remain proactive in keeping her end of the business plan running smoothly. No management by crisis, no putting out fires are allowed. I feel that being able to look beyond the functional boundaries of your department and envision the whole organizational picture is the key to keeping your input in perspective and maintaining what I call 'organizational forecasting ability.' That's why I read my company's annual reports, 10K statements, and 10Q statements, and I follow the stock performance. The administrative assistant is a right-hand function to an executive who's responsible for coordinating one department's actions with the goals of the whole company.

Candidate 3: My current job as a secretary to the vice president of investor relations entails very heavy word processing, and its broad duties consequently focus on meeting deadlines with accuracy. My present boss doesn't rely on me for screening calls, and I have an assistant who handles all the office filing. That leaves only one thing for me: heavy-duty production on my Mac. From the day I was hired, we agreed that my primary responsibility would focus on putting together mutual fund prospectuses, annual reports, and 10K filings. I work on a project-by-project basis and get a lot of satisfaction from developing a library of my work. Of course, I would welcome the opportunity to handle other tasks in addition to heavy word processing. That's why I'm so interested in this position.

Obviously, these secretaries define themselves very differently vis-à-vis their personal business missions, their ways of impacting their companies, and their relationships with their bosses.

Also, beware the candidate who replies to this query with generic lists of duties like this: "Well, I'm a secretary, so I type, answer phones, and file. What else would you like to know?" Such bulleted lists (many poor resumés, by the way, are written like this) reveal absolutely no self-confidence, pride in work, or inclination to see the broader implications of one's actions. Chances are that you'll have to drive home lessons with this person about being a team player and taking a greater interest in her own career as well as your needs.

12. What aspects of your job do you consider most crucial?

Why Ask This Question?

This query is a logical follow-up to the previous question. If the former question sets up a broad perspective of a candidate's primary and secondary responsibilities, this add-on forces specific identification of a candidate's key strengths and areas of interest. Once again, if you're hiring someone for a newly created position in your organization, and you're not sure what criteria you'll need in selecting finalists, ask this question of your first interviewees to gain clearer insight into your own needs. It should quickly provide you with concrete data regarding their current work experiences. While you view this question from the perspective that it will help you match those areas the candidate is familiar with to your opening, you should keep in mind that many job seekers are open to and capable of learning additional skills and developing new interests.

Analyzing the Response

Typical applications of this query result in lists of black and white specialty areas that either match your needs or fall short of your expectations. For example, when hiring a human resources manager, you may need someone with lots of background in compensation, benefits administration, and employee relations. If the HR manager you're currently evaluating comes from a stronger recruitment and training background, then this candidate's brand of HR management will most likely fail to provide a solution to your specific needs.

As a case in point, when the individual responds to your question regarding what she considers to be the most crucial aspects of her position, she'll initially link her ability to reduce company expenses to reduced costs per hire and a highly trained workforce—not to more competitive worker's compensation insurance premiums and reduced 401(k) plan administration fees. Consequently, you should look carefully at the candidate's initial response in order to identify her comfort zone and her plans for initially attacking the new job.

How to Get More Mileage Out of the Question. The response that the candidate generates at this juncture will typically get to the heart of his bottom-line responsibilities. Salespeople, for example, will demonstrate whether they are more money-motivated or driven to please customers regardless of the sale. Top producers who define themselves as "closers" will say that the most crucial aspect of their position lies in getting the prospect to say yes. You might come back with a retort like this: "I've found that people who define themselves as closers are often more apt to *debate* than they are to *persuade*. Therefore, they're inclined to impress clients rather than try to gain their confidence. They also sometimes have a tendency to talk when they should be listening, and they have a low tolerance for detail that makes them cut far too many corners. Could anyone ever accuse you of having any of those characteristics?"

On the other hand, a salesperson who sees the most crucial aspects of her job as developing long-term relationships with clients might avoid even mentioning closing the sale in her response. Such candidates are willing to get to the sale more slowly in an effort to gain a prospect's confidence and become an informational resource for that customer. Although these are certainly noble intentions, you might question: "I've found that people who are willing to go slowly in terms of closing the sale sometimes have an inability to distinguish sound sales approaches from ineffective ones. They can waste time on nonworkable leads by trying to win over people who are just price-shopping, and there is an inclination to be run ragged by demanding customers. Could anyone ever accuse you of having any of those characteristics?"

The purpose of these retorts is not to discourage an otherwise optimistic candidate who is secure in her style of doing business. Instead, it shows a "point-counterpoint" reverse strategy for challenging the candidate's beliefs about what she feels are the most crucial aspects of her work.

13. How many hours a week do you find it necessary to work in order to get your job done?

Why Ask This Question?

This is obviously a critical question revolving around your hidden agenda of workplace expectations: If a candidate works 8:00 A.M. to 8:00 P.M., and you happen to pride yourself on completing your daily tasks by 4:59 P.M., then your business styles don't match. You may very well reason here that overly optimistic candidates can spread themselves too thin by starting more than they could realistically hope to finish. If that's the case, you would probably view that inability to complete work in a timely and consistent manner as poor business judgment.

If you're at a stage in your career, by contrast, where you're working twelve-hour days, and you expect a new hire to keep you company, then the fact that the candidate intends to leave at 5:00 sharp may become an overwhelming obstacle because it shows a lack of dedication to the job.

Analyzing the Response

Good Answers. So what should you expect to hear in a given candidate's response? If someone has after-hour commitments via night school or a second position, then you'll probably get a direct response limiting the person's overtime commitments. In contrast, if the candidate wants your particular position at all costs, you'll most likely hear that she is willing to do whatever it takes to land the position. But what if the candidate isn't sure what your needs are? An astute candidate would probably provide you with a response that avoids limitations and keeps the lines of communication open:

> "Mr. Employer, I've worked jobs that have required unlimited time commitments on an ongoing basis, and I've worked for companies that looked down on anyone who worked beyond normal business hours. I'm capable of excelling in either type of environment. Which style do you envision for this job?"

In this case, the candidate will have bought herself some time by responding very openly to a closed-end query. She could now take an offensive position to a question that was meant to throw her into a defensive mode. Hopefully along the way you will have gained some valuable insights into this individual's plans for dedication to long office hours. After all, time in the office is often an indicator of future commitment. Remember that certain people live to work while others work to live. Those willing to dedicate long hours and sacrifice personal life for business fall into the "live to work" category, which may bode better for your business.

14. How does your position relate to the overall goals of your department or company?

Why Ask This Question?

This one is self-explanatory. If you're looking for someone who ties individual performance to the bigger picture, then this global query will be your best bet. This question can be used at the clerical or senior management level. The key to its interpretation, moreover, lies in the *degree* to which the candidate sees his own impact on areas outside of his immediate department.

Analyzing the Response

Let's take an example. Say you're interviewing candidates for a vice president of finance position. When you ask this query to a very progressive career builder (approximately in his mid-thirties, six years of experience with a Big 6 accounting firm before going inside with a client about two years ago, and MBA CPA credentials) you soon learn that this individual actually defines himself by medium-scale victories. In other words, you find out that his brand of vice presidency relies more on a heavy-handed CFO calling all the shots while he implements those decisions: It was the CFO who took the company public. The CFO created the organization's accounting and finance infrastructures. And the CFO does all the road shows presenting the company's stock to Wall Street analysts and brokers.

So you ask yourself, Where does this young vice president of finance actually make the biggest impact on his current company? And you realize that it is an implementor of someone else's decisions, not as a creator of his own strategic objectives. So if you're looking for someone with an exceptional track record for development and design of systems to lead your company's finance function, then the fact that this candidate's brand of finance has more to do with following the chief financial officer's lead will make you steer clear of this hire. It's a classical case of "able individual—wrong opportunity," and this query will hopefully have brought that issue to the surface.

On the other hand, if your CFO wants to maintain a fair amount of control over the corporate finance function, then hiring a lesser-experienced VP of finance who's used to reporting upward for ultimate sign-off on key decisions might be a very logical and prudent choice. Therefore, when assessing candidates' responses regarding how they relate their position to the overall goals of the department or company, gauge the responses with concrete examples of their responsibilities and their ultimate authority to make and enforce decisions.

15. What area of your skills do you need to improve upon in the next year?

Why Ask This Question?

Self-critical insight is a necessary trait shared by all high-performance job candidates. Without self-admitted shortcomings, a candidate will most likely require a greater deal of feedback from you about his mistakes to make sure that he learns from them. He may also border on cockiness and abrasiveness because he may be the type who finds fault in others without objectively looking at himself to find solutions to problems. In short, you may need to cultivate a greater sense of objectivity in this individual by helping him focus on *what* is right rather than being unduly concerned about *who* is right.

In comparison, candidates who openly accept their shortcomings from an objective third-party point of view will put you and your management team in a good position for damage control once those admitted weaknesses surface. The issue then becomes monitoring the new hire's performance and then adding structure and support from a positive standpoint to enhance the individual's overall effectiveness.

Analyzing the Response

Short-term, tactical goals keep people balanced and focused on their present needs. Long-term, strategic goals, in contrast, make up a vision of achievement and a framework of purpose in one's life. A very acceptable answer to a short-term, tactical query can easily focus on technical skills, since most employees at any given time can bone up on some aspect of their technical abilities. Secretaries, for example, might address their shorthand having become rusty due to scant use. Programmers might address their not being totally familiar with client server applications. Controllers might address their concerns about having limited exposure to initial public offerings if that's one of the immediate issues ahead of you. These are indeed legitimate concerns, but they are "fixable" from the standpoint of simple exposure to new systems and activities.

RED FLAGS. On the strategic side, areas for improvement become more difficult for candidates to defend. Candidates who choose the strategic route in answering this question run the risk of painting themselves into a corner and damaging their candidacy. For example, candidates might point out poor career management skills as the strategic flaw they need to improve upon. Such individuals might not have developed the necessary discipline to harness their energies toward productive ends in a well-organized, consistent, and persistent manner. As a result, they are not as far along in their careers as they would like to be.

Hence, there is a lot of job-hopping evidenced by premature "reasons for leaving" past positions. Such candidates will often address the obvious lack of career stability evident from their resumés and then emphasize their need to make a long-term commitment to the next company they join. It's your call, and it's not an easy one when taking a leap of faith that the candidate will change past patterns of behavior once a part of your company. Still, you might optimistically view this recognition as a positive sign that the individual is volunteering such a critical concern so openly.

CAUTION. The important thing is that the candidate gets invited to address tactical or strategic weaknesses and present solutions for self-improvement. Again, this holistic interviewing question tests the individual's ability to recognize flaws in judgment, past performance, career management, and the like. Beware the candidate who fails to accept your invitation to criticize himself. A lack of openness will deny the possibility for self-improvement. And anyone who shies away from self-critical insight shows little ability to learn from past mistakes. That penchant will offer little to your company, which is in turn making its own mistakes and relying on its management team to steer new courses into uncharted waters.

Four

Questions About
Career Stability

Your likelihood of objectively evaluating a candidate's potential to influence your organization rests squarely on your ability to discern the individual's motivations, values, and career goals. Employment longevity is often a function of a candidate's reason for leaving past positions—the link in the individual's career progression. Our simple premise here is that people tend to repeat patterns of change in their careers over time. Therefore, if you can identify what trips a candidate's internal job change mechanism, you'll learn two things:

1. The person's capacity for making long-term commitments
2. Whether the opportunity that you offer will satisfy the individual's needs

Accordingly, the key to determining the slippery issue of candidate career motivations will lie in examining the most important line on an employment application: the reason for leaving.

Aggressively probing a candidate's motivation for changing past positions will address the "motivation behind the moves" that drives the individual's career philosophy. Your ability to account for these *silent motives* will spell success or failure in the candidate selection process because reasons for leaving are the clearest indicators of a person's career motivations, realistic goals, and tolerance for adversity. They consequently reveal the true person behind all the hype.

Of course, the swift changes in economic cycles after the merger and acquisition craze of the 1980s followed by widespread economic stagnation in the early 1990s have blurred the lines of measurement for employee longevity and loyalty. You obviously don't want to hold it against candidates if they were caught up in layoffs beyond their control. Your goal, consequently, will be to distinguish between candidates who were laid off through no fault of their own and those who purposely orchestrated their own moves.

Qualifying the Layoff

Unprecedented layoffs have plagued corporate America for two decades and indiscriminately and adversely affected many very hard-working individuals who happened to be in the wrong division or department of an underperforming company. Slashing of balance sheets meant that thousands of workers could be cut from the payroll simultaneously. And many disenfranchised workers witnessed a "breach of the American dream" wherein increased corporate profitability stemmed from job slashing, watered-down benefits, and depressed wages. Worst of all, complementing this new harsh economic reality was the traditional belief that anyone laid off was a poor performer or underachiever.

On the other hand, not all layoffs occur because of massive divisional downsizings. It is also the case that "layoff" for too many workers has become a convenient umbrella excuse for glossing over individual failures. People unable to reinvent their jobs in light of their companies' changing needs are often simply displaced nowadays. Rather than structuring progressive disciplinary measures to eventually justify terminating the worker, employers decide on a no-fault layoff and agree to pay unemployment compensation and write a letter of recommendation. Your first step in qualifying any "downsizing," therefore, is to distinguish between individual and group layoffs.

16. How many employees were laid off simultaneously?

Why Ask This Question?

This query focuses the candidate on his former company's actions and automatically links his layoff to a particular business need. If the candidate was individually laid off (and possibly "fired"), there was probably a reason why he was chosen to leave. It may simply be a matter of tenure: the LIFO (last-in, first-out) method dictates that employees with the least amount of tenure be let go first. However, that's typically the only occasion where the individual layoff is justified. Shy of that scenario, workers who are laid off individually are many times jettisoned for lack of production, interpersonal problems, or core competencies and requisite technical skills that have become obsolete.

Analyzing the Response

How to Get More Mileage Out of the Question. When a candidate is indeed individually laid off, you'll want to ask these questions:

"Was it logical for you to be the individual chosen to be laid off? How so?"

"Could your individual layoff possibly have been related to your performance or level of production and output?"

"Is there anything your boss didn't know about your performance that could have perhaps changed her mind about choosing you to begin the layoff process?"

"Was anyone else laid off immediately after you were? If so, how many, and from what departments?"

"Do you feel that the decision to let you go had anything to do with your interpersonal relationships with your boss or any of your coworkers? Could politics have adversely affected you?"

A second corollary that relates to qualifying the layoff and that mirrors this query is:

17. How many people survived the cut?

Why Ask This Question?

The phrasing of this question allows the candidate to assess the layoff from a different business angle, namely the organization's need to retain certain people to keep the work flowing. As such, it complements the preceding query by forcing the candidate to objectively come to terms with her past company's actions. Furthermore, the response you get should again link this individual's fate to an objective business reason for having been let go.

Analyzing the Response

How to Get More Mileage Out of the Question. If a particular department or division was eliminated, then the only people who survived were outside of those ill-fated areas. Again, that's totally beyond a candidate's control and shouldn't weigh as a negative swing factor in the selection process. However, if the individual was laid off from a department that is still intact, there may have been a problem.

Therefore, ask the individual to account for why particular individuals survived the cut:

"How did the organization decide who in the marketing department would remain and who would be let go?"

"What criteria were used in determining your department's new staffing configuration?"

"Were you surprised to find out that anyone in particular was kept or let go, or did the layoffs occur as you expected?"

Inviting candidates to assess how the company decided to "dismantle" a particular business unit will provide you with insights into their abilities to view problem areas with global objectivity. You'll also see if they react negatively and personally to unfavorable outcomes in their lives.

Finally, a third issue for qualifying a layoff lies in asking:

18. How many waves of layoffs did you survive before you were let go yourself?

Why Ask This Question?

Surviving multiple rounds of cuts can be an exceptionally attractive attribute. Only the most consistent performers are asked to wind down an operation. And when all is said and done, not only did they stick it out in terms of helping the company through a very difficult and emotional time, but they never let up in production or output. Although they knew that their eventual reward for their efforts was nothing more than their own layoff, they found new ways of adding value in light of their organizations' changing needs. As a matter of fact, this is often one of the first issues that contingency recruiters mention to prospective employers in the candidate presentation process. After all, helping businesses wind down their operations usually spells both loyalty and high performance.

Analyzing the Response

How to Get More Mileage Out of the Question. Allow interviewees the chance to explain, round by round if necessary, why they were chosen to stay aboard as others were let go. How many hats did they have to wear to keep their jobs through those layoffs? Where did they receive their cross-functional training? How did they cross-train their peers? What prompted their managers to choose them to help wind things down, and how did those managers solicit their support? You'll be surprised at what valuable information you could develop in examining a candidate's approach to aid an organization's downsizing.

Keep in mind as well that there is a difference between Chapter 7 and Chapter 11 bankruptcies. Chapter 7 total liquidations leave no survivors: there's typically only the carcass of a company left. Chapter 11 bankruptcies, on the other hand, are restructurings where the courts hold creditors at bay to give companies a chance to raise revenues to a point where they can eventually emerge out of bankruptcy. In those situations, a core staff of employees remains to carry on the business. As you guessed, it could be a very big plus in a candidate's column to be among this core of survivors mandated with returning the organization to profitability.

How do you document this information during your interview? Simply by taking notes explaining the circumstances surrounding each layoff. For instance, if the candidate writes "Layoff" in the "reason for leaving" space at the last job, jot down your "qualified" reason for the layoff as shown by the examples in Figure 4-1.

Obviously the answers you'll generate might open a whole new can of worms in terms of the individual's suitability at your firm. And that's exactly what delving into these reasons for leaving is supposed to do! At the very least, gathering this type of information on the front end will point out which areas need to be more fully explored through the use of a reference check a little further down the road. Congratulations—you've just learned to dramatically enhance your candidate evaluation skills!

These three questions should provide you with invaluable insights into one of the most overlooked areas in candidate evaluation: qualifying the layoff. Now remember, however, that there is another type of reason for leaving that you'll want to examine to gain a thorough feel for candidates' goals and motivations: namely, when individuals deliberately make their own moves.

Qualifying Individually Orchestrated Moves

Although movement from company to company can happen for very good reasons, too much movement in a candidate's background—especially when it's movement for movement's sake—should throw up a red flag for you. Bearing in mind our premise that people tend to repeat patterns of change in their careers over time, you need to identify what

Figure 4-1. Qualifying and documenting layoffs as a candidate's reason for leaving past companies.

> Layoff: Company underwent Chapter 7 total liquidation.
>
> Layoff: Company underwent Chapter 11 restructuring: 300 employees reduced to 60. Only loan origination division kept while loan servicing portfolio was sold off to another bank. Loan servicing staff totally let go.
>
> Staff reduction: West Coast pharmaceutical manufacturing division relocated to corporate HQ in Chicago. Candidate unable to relocate for family reasons.
>
> Layoff: Four people let go out of a staff of 18. LIFO (last-in, first-out) syndrome: candidate had only one year of tenure.
>
> Downsizing: Candidate individually laid off. Feels it's because her boss personally disliked her.
>
> Layoff: Candidate individually laid off. Never quite felt like she belonged due to a corporate culture mismatch. Left on bad terms. Employer probably won't give a reference.

trips a candidate's internal job change mechanism. The most effective way to do that is by challenging the most hackneyed and overused excuse in corporate America: "no room for growth."

"No room for growth" translates into bored, tired, and unmotivated. Unfortunately, too many job candidates wear it as a badge of honor showing that they've mastered and consequently outgrown their positions. After emerging from the largest economic contraction since the 1930s, how much advancement and growth should job candidates realistically expect? The 1980s dogma of career development was supplanted by the concept of "keeping your job" once the bombs fell in Iraq in January of 1991. And it's certainly not a conservative economic prognostication to reveal to you that job scarcity will remain the law of the land in light of the repatterning of America's corporate fabric: the specter of increased taxes as a means of deficit reduction, the impending changes in health care coverage, the Baby Bust generation's inadequate demand for consumer loans, the fallout of the military-industrial complex, technology explosions, and fierce global competition make the entrance into the third millennium insecure at best. So please . . . spare me your frustration at not being challenged or rewarded enough at work!

Therefore, when faced with a generic "no room for growth" reason for leaving, ask the individual:

19. What does growth mean to you?

Why Ask This Question?

"Growth" is one of those slippery words in the job-hunting world. To some, it means (vertical) promotions up the ladder. To others, it means increased responsibilities gained through (lateral) broadened experiences. To still others, it simply means more money. Don't assume that you know a candidate's true motives when "no room for growth" is the stated reason for leaving. Instead, use this as an opportunity to gauge how realistic the candidate is, what true motives exist, and how much capacity for dealing with adversity the person has.

Analyzing the Response

How to Get More Mileage Out of the Question. Let's role-play this one together. I'll be the candidate; you be the interviewer.

Situation 1

Employer: Paul, I see that you marked "no room for growth" as your reason for wishing to leave your present company. What exactly does growth mean to you?

Candidate: Well, I really want to work in an organization where I can make a difference. I'm not looking for quick advances and promotions up the proverbial ladder, but I do want to know that my contribution has a positive impact on my company. My present company is an excellent organization in terms of the tenure of its senior management team, but it's exactly that paradox of tenure that creates a corporate culture that refuses to keep up with the times. Besides, it's a mature company in a descending life cycle. I see working for your firm as an opportunity to join a dynamic company with a lot more risk and a lot more reward. And it's exactly that risk-reward relationship that makes me feel that I could hit a home run by joining your firm.

Well, what do you think? I don't know about you, but I'm sold! I understand this candidate's career goals, and I also understand how those goals would naturally be met by joining my company. This person passed this hurdle. Let's look at another example.

Situation 2

Employer: Paul, I see that you marked "no room for growth" as your reason for leaving your last company. What exactly does growth mean to you?

Candidate: As a senior vice president of loan servicing, I'm overseeing a loan service portfolio of 100,000 loans worth approximately $10 billion. We've built that up from 10,000 loans worth about $1 billion nine years ago. If we were still on an aggressive expansion track, Ms. Employer, I wouldn't be in your office today. But our bank was recently bought out by a huge finance company that put us on its balance sheet simply to diversify its portfolio. Accordingly, the word's out that we're going into a mode of maintenance and stasis.

Working with your company would allow me to oversee a significantly larger portfolio—450,000 loans worth about $45 billion. And that would just about allow me to reach the brass ring in my career. I'm ready for that level of responsibility, and I'm hungry to make it happen. That's why I'm here today.

Now what do you think? Yes, I agree! This candidate has a very legitimate motivation to make a job change, and I admire his awareness of his accomplishments and realistic self-assessment of his ability to contribute. He passes this test.

Situation 3

Employer: Paul, I see that you marked "no room for growth" as your reason for leaving your last company. What exactly does growth mean to you?

Candidate: I would say that growth means having the opportunity to make more money based on my contribution to the organization. I need a challenge. I also need to know that my ideas are supported by senior management. After all, if you're not going to be appreciated for doing your job day in and day out, why bother? I'm not saying that the owners of my present company owe me a living, but their management style is sorely lacking in that they just don't seem to care. There are simply too many problems at that company, and they can't seem to get their act together. As a matter of fact, a number of people are looking to make a move right now. That's why I left. . . .

Okay, I set you up! I know you realize that situation 3 is a problem candidate. But why? Besides the whiny attitude, why is this candidate a poor risk?

There are two reasons. First, he lacks a critical quality that sets high-performance career candidates apart from the rest: the ability to remain an objective, third-party evaluator of his career. What's important to him is what his company can do for him—not what he can do for his company. He's subjectively and emotionally entangled in a situation that he refuses to try to change. In his response, he never addresses his attempts to confront the problems that are making that organization (in his opinion, at least) stall. It's exactly that lack of trying which makes him appear whiny and complaining.

Second, and even more significant, keep in mind that whatever problems made a candidate decide to leave his last job must be solved by your company. If you can't offer him a solution to his problems, then there's no reason why his joining your firm would make for a more successful outcome. His problem is that he's simply not motivated at his present job, and there's no reason to believe that a new situation will make him act any differently. After all, he'll be expected to motivate himself once aboard your company. Additionally, your organization, like all others, has its own "dysfunctionality quotient." Since he's only a taker and not a giver, you'll have nothing to offer this gentleman once the novelty of the new job wears off six months down the line. Consequently, he's probably got nothing to offer you. Move on to your next interview.

20. What will you do differently at your present company if you don't get this position?

Why Ask This Question?

If a candidate's response to "What does growth mean to you?" appears self-centered or shows lack of global reasoning, but the individual otherwise shows promise, then press the issue further. Force the candidate to come to terms with how she'll make her work life more palatable once she returns to reality back in the office. Look again for creative ways in which a double benefit will result both for candidate and company. After all, practically any situation can be enhanced with a renewed commitment to success, whether at the company, department, or coworker level. Besides, even if the candidate isn't wholeheartedly committed to bettering her employment relationship, she should at least be smart

Figure 4-2. Realistic reasons for candidates orchestrating their own moves to leave companies.

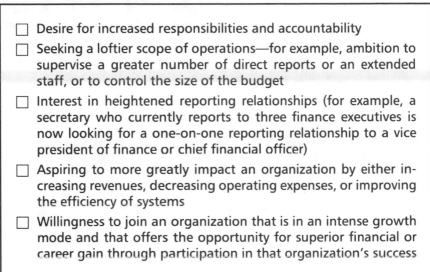

☐ Desire for increased responsibilities and accountability

☐ Seeking a loftier scope of operations—for example, ambition to supervise a greater number of direct reports or an extended staff, or to control the size of the budget

☐ Interest in heightened reporting relationships (for example, a secretary who currently reports to three finance executives is now looking for a one-on-one reporting relationship to a vice president of finance or chief financial officer)

☐ Aspiring to more greatly impact an organization by either increasing revenues, decreasing operating expenses, or improving the efficiency of systems

☐ Willingness to join an organization that is in an intense growth mode and that offers the opportunity for superior financial or career gain through participation in that organization's success

enough to show you that she's a team player willing to put her company's needs ahead of her own.

Analyzing the Response

Caution Beware the respondent who refuses to entertain this issue. If life is so bad back at the office that nothing can salvage even parts of that employment relationship, then you're looking at a "mentally unemployed" individual who has perhaps given up too easily on fixing problems in his career. In such cases, the response (or lack thereof) should suffice to convince you that the candidate doesn't belong in your company.

By the way, many employers consider it a major "ding" against a candidate when the person leaves a job without having another position firmly in hand. It points to a lack of business maturity and a low tolerance for adversity when an employee unseats herself without another firm offer of employment secured. In today's employment marketplace, it's hard to believe that conditions are so bad that people would rather go on unemployment than wait it out at their present jobs while looking for a new one. Besides, they should know that their marketability goes way down when they're in transition as opposed to when they're employed. It's a rookie mistake, and it shows a lack of business savvy.

Therefore, knowing how to effectively press the "no room for growth" issue in your selection interview will clearly reveal an individual's career values and motivations—a critical insight into the person's ability to make an impact on your company. Now that you've examined the pros and cons of candidates who have orchestrated their own moves from company to company, look at the brief checklist of favorable reasons for leaving shown in Figure 4-2. Again, when you know what you're looking for, it makes the whole recruitment and selection process that much easier.

Five

Searching for Patterns of Progression Through the Ranks

A critical characteristic of high-performance job candidates may be found in individuals' progression through the ranks. *People who show progressive demonstrations of increased responsibilities understand how to add value to their companies over time.* These are the proven performers who are capable of reinventing their jobs and assuming responsibilities above and beyond the call of duty. The fact that their achievements have been noticed and rewarded by their superiors makes these individuals capable of contributing to your organization over the long haul. (Promotion through the ranks, after all, is usually a function of longevity: You have to stay long enough in a company to receive recognition and added responsibilities.)

There's a unique way to bring out a candidate's progression through the ranks during the interview process. Most employers begin an interview by asking, "So, Janet, tell me about what you do on your present job." Yes, that's an icebreaker, and it should get the candidate talking freely. However, the information you derive from asking that question adds little value to your meeting: You simply end up getting a laundry list of duties that are already highlighted in the resumé. Also, you typically end up with only a generic job description that would fit anyone with that person's title.

Instead, try opening the question by using a "progression indicator" that invites candidates to describe their present duties in light of their historical advancement:

21. Describe how you've progressed through the ranks and landed in your current position at ABC Company.

Why Ask This Question?

This technique adds a historical context or perspective to the individual's current duties. Instead of simply focusing on her responsibilities as an accounting manager, for example, the candidate would address her various promotions leading up to her accounting managership role. All of a sudden, you've got a much deeper understanding of this individual's abilities to assume broader responsibilities via her progression through the ranks.

Analyzing the Response

Remember, many job candidates don't reveal progression on a resumé. Instead, they simply list their last position held at each company. So if you don't ask for the history leading up to the person's present job, you'll lose that added dimension of progression. Here's how it works. Imagine you're sitting down with an accounting manager whose resumé shows that she oversees a staff of eight people in payables, receivables, and payroll. Asking the question, "So, Janet, tell me about your present job as accounting manager" will reveal the following information, which you jot down in your notepad:

- Oversees 8 in A/P, A/R; general ledger; multistate payroll in 7 Western states for 100 employees
- ADP-generated quarterly tax reporting
- A/P = $12MM/mo; A/R = $14MM/mo
- Reports to controller; dotted-line reporting relationship to VP Finance

That's not bad information in terms of gathering technical reporting data and scope of responsibilities. But most of that information is probably already on the resumé or employment application. So what clearer insights have you gained into this candidate's abilities to influence your company's future? Unfortunately, not too much. You have nothing more than historical facts.

How to Get More Mileage Out of the Question. Now, let's see how this can become more valuable and telling simply by asking the question differently using the progression indicator: "So, Janet, describe how you've progressed through the ranks and landed in your current position at ABC Company." Janet's feedback sounds something like this:

> "Well, I began with the organization six years ago as a staff accountant. I did that job for about three years, but in that time my supervisor relied on me to handle a lot of work in his absence. I guess I took on what I'd call a team leader role in terms of running the office in his absence, and people generally came to me with the tougher questions that no one else seemed to be able to answer.
>
> After that, I was promoted to accounting supervisor and did that for the next two and a half years. The accounting supervisor to whom I originally reported left for an early retirement. He determined that I would be his logical replacement, and I was very happy to receive that promotion.
>
> Finally, about six months ago, we had some turnover, and the controller asked me to take on additional responsibilities as accounting manager. Since then, I've been overseeing a staff of eight people in accounts payable, accounts receivable, and payroll. I report directly to the controller with a dotted-line relationship to the vice president of finance, and I helped take our company through a software conversion that we completed just last month. . . ."

Do you hear the difference that the progression indicator makes? You'll still end up with a thorough understanding of Janet's current primary and secondary responsibilities, reporting relationships, and scope of authority. But now you have time frames and accomplishments by which to measure them. In taking your notes on her employment application, your comments would look something like this:

1. Staff accountant (3 years)—assumed team leader responsibilities
2. Accounting supervisor ($2^1/_2$ years)—after incumbent retired
3. Accounting manager (6 months)—asked by controller to oversee staff of 8 in A/P, A/R, and payroll; general ledger; directly reports to controller; dotted-line to VP Finance

Historically reframing a candidate's career progression will add new insights and dimensions to your evaluation. It should make your life easier when recommending this candidate to another member of your organization. And it will certainly facilitate your hiring decision seeing that another employer in a different company placed that much value in this individual.

But what if the candidate wasn't on her last job long enough to progress vertically through the ranks? Or what if she was there for six years and held the same job title over that entire period of time? Should that be held against her? If you ask a candidate to detail her historical progression over time and you get a response saying, "Well, I started as an accounting manager, so I didn't really progress anywhere," then follow up your initial question like this:

22. How have you added value to your job over time?

Why Ask This Question?

Every employee in America is hired to achieve one of three benefits for a company: either to (1) increase revenues, (2) decrease expenses, or (3) save time. Although vertical progression through the ranks is admirable, long-term commitment to one position is equally necessary in running a successful business. Still, no job remains static over time, and phrasing your question this way forces candidates to account for the changes necessary to maintain output or increase production.

Analyzing the Response

How to Get More Mileage Out of the Question. Candidates may struggle with this question because it's so broad. When that's the case, question how the company, division, or department has changed over time. When a company is rapidly expanding, for example, revenues typically have to be maintained for an extended period before full-time staff is added to accommodate the greater workload. Consequently, productivity per employee must increase to produce more product with the same number of people. Reciprocally, when companies are downsizing, employees lucky enough to survive a layoff are typically forced to maintain the work flow with fewer staff members to support their efforts. Once again, we have a case for increased productivity per employee.

In either case, framing candidates' "value-added" achievements around a changing business environment will usually aid those individuals in redefining how work was redistributed to meet increased production demands or how work was reallocated because of new staffing configurations. By examining how the company had to change over time, candidates should find it easier to address their roles in the unit's new direction.

To delve further into this issue, you should ask candidates to address specific steps taken to reach their unit's production goals. In this case, follow up your question about added value like this:

23. How have you had to reinvent or redefine your job to meet your company's changing needs? What pro-active steps did you have to take to increase the output of your position?

Why Ask This Question?

Phrasing the follow-up question this ways forces candidates to see themselves in terms of the company's bottom line. The ability to increase revenues or decrease costs is an absolute litmus test of an employee's track record of influencing an organization. Many people fall into the routine of going to work and performing a job. They consequently lose perspective about the bigger picture. Therefore, crafting a question that forces individuals to account for their "macro" impact in their immediate area of responsibility forces them to come to terms with their value as corporate assets or as "human resources."

Analyzing the Response

How to Get More Mileage Out of the Question. Asking people how they've added value to their companies by reinventing their jobs over time is indeed a challenging query. There's usually an uncomfortable moment of silence when candidates ponder a question that seems to offer meaning to everything they do in the working world, but that they'd never thought of before. And so after a few shuffles in the chair and awkward clearings of the throat, generalities come spewing forth regarding their commitment, dependability, and dedication. Those fluff adjectives do little, however, in terms of generating the concrete information you want.

"Nice try," you might say, smiling, "but that's not what I mean." Give them a moment to regain their composure and continue with such questions as:

"How did your role as an accounting manager change over time?"

"Were you the architect of your changing responsibilities, or did your immediate supervisor direct your revised focus?"

"In terms of your company's changing needs, did your department take on a new mission? And if so, what was your role in redefining your department's new direction?"

"Would you say that the scope of your responsibility increased or decreased in terms of the size of the staff you oversaw or the budget under your control?"

And so goes the questioning pattern. It's a challenge indeed for candidates to articulate their overall capabilities to make a positive impact on an organization, as opposed to performing the day-to-day generic duties that earn them a paycheck. You'll no doubt experience some of them walking away from your interview scratching their heads about their roles in business. Of course, not all positions in all companies require high levels of self-esteem and global reasoning abilities. Still, when you need a superstar candidate for a demanding position, this should help you identify individuals who look proactively at their own performance and find ways to increase the work flow and efficiently streamline operations.

Bear in mind that there are two types of progression in people's career histories: Individuals either assume greater responsibilities and move vertically up the ladder with higher titles and pay, or they horizontally expand their jobs by assuming broader responsibilities. In the latter case, although candidates retain the same title, their broadened responsibilities add a depth of knowledge and experience to the company (and to their resumés!). To amplify both types of career changes, ask:

24. Distinguish between your vertical progression through the ranks at your last/present company and your lateral assumption of broader responsibilities.

Why Ask This Question?

It's fairly well known that American organizations are flattening out by reducing the levels of management necessary to carry out business. Consequently, far fewer jobs are available up the proverbial corporate ladder. Instead, many workers are seeking cross-functional experiences to broaden their expertise of their organizations' line units. Similarly, many executives are looking for international assignments to gain the broader knowledge of doing business overseas.

Analyzing the Response

As discussed under Question 21, documenting vertical promotions is a fairly straightforward task. The key to evaluating lateral movement, on the other hand, lies in understanding the candidate's motivation behind those moves. When workers assume broader responsibilities by relocating to another plant or related business unit, it is either at their request or the company's. Both reasons are telling.

How to Get More Mileage Out of the Question. Employees who deliberately seek out cross-functional opportunities will most likely increase their chances for promotion later on at their current firm, or they will improve their marketability elsewhere. The answer regarding the individual's motivation can be gleaned by asking something like:

"When you switched from field human resources to corporate human resources, what ultimate goal did you have in mind?"

"And what prompted the move: Were you asked by management to transfer to the corporate office, or did you put in for the transfer yourself?"

"In retrospect, what was the ultimate benefit to the company?"

Employees who relocate or take on lateral assignments at the company's request show both loyalty and flexibility—two very admirable traits in today's business world. After all, what greater test of an employee's commitment is there than accepting an assignment overseas for a year and relocating the entire family? Moreover, in a recent study conducted by the national outplacement firm Right Associates in conjunction with the University of Tennessee, it was estimated that 41 percent of employee relocations were for lateral moves whereas only 39 percent were for promotions.[1] Consequently, there is a marked shift away from the traditionally accepted "transfer equals promotion" paradigm. What that means to you is that lateral relocations and cross-functional training represent a new barometer for measuring employee commitment and adaptability.

1. Right Associates and the University of Tennessee, "Valuing the Dual Career Work Force: Business Implications for Spouse Employment Issues in Relocation" (research study, Knoxville, Tenn., 1995), p. 6.

Discussing the ramifications of individuals' career movements within their companies can clearly serve as an accurate indicator of people's needs and motivation. It's equally important to look at career progression from a job change perspective as candidates consider leaving their current company to join yours. When employed candidates interview with you and express a generic reason for wanting to leave their present position like, "I'm looking for added responsibilities and more challenge," it's time to gain a more accurate understanding of their *real* motivation for change. You can gather a more realistic response by asking:

25. What would be your next logical move in progression at your present company?

Why Ask This Question?

Let's face it: No one wants to talk about a derailed career. After all, upward movers and fast trackers will stay with a company as long as they can still make a positive impact on the organization and their interpersonal relationships remain strong. Once that win-win relationship gets compromised, however, the job search begins. Still, as a savvy and sophisticated interviewer, you're responsible for getting to the heart of the matter, and few questions work as well as this one in forcing individuals to candidly come to terms with their current limitations.

Analyzing the Response

The "next logical move in progression" query surfaces candidates' immediate career goals: namely, their next step in added responsibilities, influence, and compensation. Something is blocking their attainment of that brass ring—a superior who refuses to retire, a change in senior management that threatens job stability, or a level of achievement that seems to elude them—and they may not be comfortable admitting it to themselves, much less you, the prospective employer.

How to Get More Mileage Out of the Question. A gentle probing question regarding the nature of this career block might sound something like this: "Chuck, the company is healthy, your track record with the firm is apparently very solid, yet you're looking outside for increased opportunities. Share with me what's blocking the road ahead for you. And what would have to happen for you to remove that roadblock from your path?" Your caring tone should go a long way in encouraging the candidate to open up regarding his actual concerns. More importantly, your targeted question will have pierced a wound that you have every right to explore before passing final judgment on this individual's candidacy.

To encourage the candidate further, you might ask questions like these:

> "Where exactly on the organization chart would you be if you made one vertical move upward?"

> "Whose job would you have, why would you want it, and what would you typically have to do to get there?"

> "What would you have to add to your background to receive that promotion?"

> "How long would it take for you to see that game plan through to completion?"

> "From a relationship standpoint with your boss, what's the key factor keeping you from reaching that rung on the ladder?"

RED FLAGS. All shooting stars eventually burn out. Interpersonal relationships fluctuate as personnel changes take place. And the heir apparent to the throne may get passed over for someone else who is possibly less capable but more politically fit. These are all natural occurrences that encourage workers to explore opportunities with other teams in different leagues. You are ultimately responsible, however, for ensuring that the malady plaguing the candidate isn't chronic and going to carry forward to your company.

When you're not sure that you're getting the whole story regarding the candidate's motivation for leaving the current company and joining yours, apply the "pressure-temperament-recognition" triad to explore common problem areas that candidates usually prefer to hide from prospective employers. These three issues should be applied as rapid-fire queries to swiftly identify a candidate's "hot buttons" that could trigger negative reactions. A dubious response in any of the three following areas should be probed more deeply for fear that the problem will infect new employees in your organization. For example, you could use this questioning strategy as follows:

> "Vic, I sense that you're holding back from me regarding what's really standing in your way at your current company.

Tell me about the level of *pressure* on your job: Did you ever find yourself complaining about management's inability or unwillingness to relieve the pressure, and could that have anything to do with your decision to look elsewhere?

Would you say that your *temperament* complemented your boss's, or were you cut from a different cloth? In other words, did the interpersonal relationship with your immediate superior demotivate you or encourage you to reach your personal best?

How could the company have done a better job of *recognizing* your contributions?"

How could these problem issues carry over into your organization? Someone who complains about management's unwillingness to better the working environment is most likely conditioned to place blame on the organization rather than accept responsibility for the company's shortcomings. In addition, having a different outlook or opinion than your supervisor is in itself no great sin, but this query may trigger some deep resentments that the candidate holds against his superior. Thus your specific mention of this issue could open a floodgate of complaints against the person's boss. Finally, feeling inadequately recognized for your contributions isn't at all uncommon—unless the candidate placed unrealistic expectations or demands on his previous company.

In short, these rapid-fire queries could very well release pent-up tensions lying just below the surface. A candidate with chronic issues regarding stress, interpersonal relationships with the boss, or the need for praise and recognitionmay very well stir up similar latent feelings in co-workers. Again, many candidates have such issues to some degree, but if they seem disproportionately strong, proceed with caution!

Six

Likability Equals Compatibility: Matching Candidates' Personalities to Your Organization's Corporate Culture

Statistically, about 80 percent of all hires in corporate America are based on a personality match—how well the two people get along and immediately establish rapport with each other. We all tend to hire in our own image, so when we see someone who appears to think and act as we do, we often build a case in our minds for finding reasons to make that placement happen. Our immediate comfort and confidence create a feeling that this person will bring out the best in us and that work will become a lot more bearable with a soul mate to share the burden.

Sometimes we see candidates that we admire for having achieved accomplishments that we wish we had ourselves, so we become inclined to delve more deeply into their backgrounds to see how they attained that brass ring that's eluded us thus far. Maybe the person graduated from Harvard. Perhaps the individual has an MBA in finance which still only remains a distant dream for you. Or possibly he worked at a very high-profile company where you always wanted to work. Whatever the cause of these immediate attractions and affinities, it is important to understand that these are all totally natural human responses that bond us to others very quickly.

Unfortunately, too many managers in business today use this likability factor as the prime criterion for bringing someone aboard. They regretfully admit later down the road that they "felt it in their gut" that a certain candidate would make a successful contribution to the company,

only to find out later that the person's management approach or technical orientation wasn't compatible with their style or the organization's
needs. So is it wrong to hire on the basis of initial gut feelings and personal affinities? Absolutely not. But it is certainly a mistake to make decisions solely on a likability factor without employing other diagnostic,
more objective tools in the selection process.

The purpose of this topic is to supply you with such diagnostic, impersonal tools to help you clearly delineate your needs and a candidate's
potential solution to the immediate challenges you're facing. Therefore,
you're cautioned to rely on your gut feelings only *after* you've objectively
diagnosed the candidate. The bottom line to keeping your gut feelings
in check is that initial *likability* must be matched by future *compatibility*—compatible business styles, management techniques, and tolerance
capacities. Then, once you've determined the individual's approach to
work, you could evaluate where you'll complement each other and balance each other out.

26. What kind of mentoring and training style do you have? Do you naturally delegate responsibilities, or do you expect your direct reports to come to you for added responsibilities?

Why Ask This Question?

Some people inherently have a high level of interest in training and
motivating others. They are "naturals" at teaching and derive a "psychic
income" from sharing their expertise and helping others grow. These
types of managers often speak of the excellent mentors that guided them
through their own careers, and they now see a chance to give back to
others what was so generously given to them—time, patience, and guidance. Other managers readily admit to having little patience for holding
others' hands. They are independent types who expect their direct reports
to operate solo. Whatever the case, you can often gauge this personal
orientation via the individual's willingness to delegate responsibilities
downward.

Analyzing the Response

Compatibility in the staff development area is critical because coworkers in discord about the amount of time to spend mentoring others

will sooner or later have a falling out. Training is the largest drain on time in business, and if you disagree with someone you hire about the priority level that staff training should receive, then you'll more than likely be at odds regarding project completion dates and work flow continuity.

In general, there are two types of delegators in business. People who are more control-oriented typically have a need to hold onto their possessions—whether that be power, information, or authority. They are very often uncomfortable passing responsibility down the line for fear that they will later be challenged by a subordinate with ideas for getting things done differently. Perhaps there is a fear that if they do not hold all the cards at any given point in time, they may be faced with a question to which they have no answer—obviously an uncomfortable position that would test anyone's feelings of insecurity. Of course, these traits don't necessarily make anyone a bad manager; they just make it more difficult for subordinates to exert autonomy and independent decision making.

Reciprocally, individuals who consistently pass responsibilities down the line—and who operate from more of a shared, participatory management style based on consensus building—naturally offer subordinates more opportunities for creative self-expression and empowerment. Such managers often employ policies of openness in information sharing, a greater sense of partnership with their coworkers, and increased accountability.

Still, you have to be aware that managers who too readily pass responsibilities down the line may sometimes be criticized for delegating work that rightfully belongs on their own desks. In addition, you could end up with chaos on your hands by injecting this type of manager into a department that needs more autocratic rules: Decentralized power placed into the hands of a loosely formed, immature team of workers will necessitate that you step in to impose the discipline that the team lacks. In short, you'll end up managing a high-need problem unit with a departmental head who is not well suited to that team's needs.

Again, there is no right or wrong delegation style, but simply a level of success associated with that manager's ability to motivate and empower staff to reach a department's goals. If this question successfully delivers the information you want, you'll be better able to identify various types of managerial candidates: those who keep their people on a short leash and who oversee even the most minute aspects of a given project, and those who expect their people to assume additional responsibilities without asking permission. That is, you'll differentiate the more autocratic controller (who will guarantee a targeted output) from the enlightened manager (capable of creating an empowered, creative worker team). Both brands of management may dedicate themselves to making your company more efficient and profitable; it's simply a matter of how to get there.

27. Every company has its own quirks—its "dysfunctionality quotient," so to speak. How dysfunctional was your last company, and how much tolerance do you have for dealing with a company's shortcomings and inconsistencies?

Why Ask This Question?

Tolerance for a company's shortcomings and inconsistencies is definitely an area that calls for compatible business styles. If you're fairly patient and realize that the hands of time turn slowly, then matching yourself up with a bull in a china closet who's used to issuing mandates that force immediate change will probably irritate both of you pretty quickly. You'll feel that she's too aggressive and makes overly optimistic assumptions by overcommitting herself. She'll feel that you're much too laid back and lack the necessary sense of urgency to steer the ship in a new direction.

Signs of dysfunction within a company include an overactive grapevine, compartmentalization, the need for total control, a deterioration of company ethics, isolation by function, and cynicism. Every company shares these characteristics at any given time—only the *degree* of dysfunctionality varies. Engaging a candidate to objectively address these corporate weaknesses demands that the individual ride a fine line between outright, subjective criticism and an objective, evaluative critique of organizational shortcomings. With this question, you'll want to assess the candidate's insights into the problems he's faced battling bureaucracy as well as the solutions he's provided in attempting to overcome those organizational flaws.

Analyzing the Response

RED FLAGS. If a candidate places herself in a victim posture by identifying weaknesses that negatively affected her performance, then beware this individual's capacity for dealing with adversity. As long as there are people in a company, there will be personality conflicts, power plays, weak leaders, jealous peers, and apathetic subordinates. Placing blame on the company for not controlling these universally human issues spells weakness and poor stamina on the candidate's part.

How to Get More Mileage Out of the Question. If a candidate fails to understand the point of this question and bluntly responds that his current company isn't dysfunctional at all, clarify your question by asking:

"Could your company be characterized as having an overactive grapevine? In other words, do the people standing around the water cooler know more about the power plays and machinations at the executive level than they probably should?"

or

"Do you find that departments work more independently of each other than they should? After all, without constant interaction among functional units, it's possible that not all players will be tugging in the same direction at any given time."

or

"Would you describe your senior management team as tight-fisted and autocratic, or does it have a policy of open financials and full disclosure so that employees feel that they own the company rather than just work there?"

or

"Were any particular departments or any of your immediate reports consistently cynical about working in the company? More importantly, how justified were they in their complaints?"

Not even the most balanced company will meet all of these criteria, so pointing these areas out should help communicate what you want the candidate to address.

Once you've gotten the candidate to identify an organizational shortcoming (which shouldn't be too hard after providing such a varied menu to choose from!), employ this follow-up query: "Tell me what role you played in solving some of these problems." By their very nature, organizational or cultural weaknesses are systemic issues beyond the control of any one employee. Therefore, you can't expect one person (shy of the

CEO) to have a serious impact on an organization's cultural shortcomings. Still, you may find that this person might have started a grassroots, bottom-up movement that encouraged interdepartmental communications.

For example, a sales manager who invites human resources recruiters to spend a day in the field to get a better feel for the types of challenges facing the account executives will open up the lines of communication between two otherwise isolated units. A vice president of finance who holds a management training workshop on how to read the firm's annual report likewise breaks through such barriers. And anyone who persuades other employees around the water cooler to stop spreading rumors is doing his share to better the work environment. A small step, yes, but a positive step nonetheless. And if you're cut from that same cloth and share similar beliefs, you'll complement each other's work styles and business objectives.

28. How would you describe the amount of structure, direction, and feedback that you need to excel?

Why Ask This Question?

People typically need more supervision when they're new to a company and learning the ins and outs of new computer systems, work styles, and company expectations. Once they've completed their initial ninety days or even first year, they naturally become more self-confident and independent. Still, some folks really thrive on feedback for a job well done. No matter how long they've held their current position, they need that ongoing pat on the back to bolster their morale and keep them on track. Others truly resent any kind of structured, ongoing feedback, believing that the supervisor's close attention implies that they're not self-sufficient on their jobs. Few areas of compatibility are as critical and immediately evident as this issue regarding feedback and structure.

Analyzing the Response

How to Get More Mileage Out of the Question. Eighty percent of respondents will say that they want a combination of feedback and independence. After all, no worker really wants a boss who will oversee every aspect of every step of a given project. That would make any of us feel paranoid about our work and limited in our abilities because of lack of trust. On the other hand, all of us like praise for a job well done and, from time to time, concrete feedback regarding our performance.

Because so many candidates will fall into this generic and comfortable answer, you need to force the issue to the extremes to really get at the candidate's true feelings regarding supervisory feedback. If necessary, reword the question this way:

> "Mary, if you had to choose between one extreme or the other, would you want a manager who totally leaves you alone to get your work done independently and only wants to hear from you if there's a problem, or would you prefer someone who meets with you regularly to help you focus on your production goals for the day or for the week?"

Again, there are no right or wrong answers: It's simply a matter of gauging your "compatibility ratio." If you're more of a career mentor and you take pride in growing your people, then you'll probably want a more intimate relationship with a subordinate because you'll want to measure the person's progress and contribute to his growth. On the other hand, if you're a hands-off manager and don't particularly relish the thought of helping staff members find their way through the woods, then a candidate who wants extra time from you will probably appear to be a high-need employee. Find this one out before you say "I do" to anyone you'll be spending long hours with—it's worth the effort on the front end inviting individuals to assess their expectations of your time.

29. In terms of managing your staff, do you "expect" more than you "inspect," or vice versa?

Why Ask This Question?

Expectation versus inspection—if that doesn't conjure up a picture of a candidate's management philosophy! As you guessed, there's nothing wrong with either style. It's simply a matter of matching the candidate's natural inclinations to your departmental needs. A fairly disorganized unit with a majority of neophytes will benefit from a general who inspects a lot. A mature team of independent technicians or artists will benefit more from a management style of freedom and creativity so that, as long as deadlines are met, the workers have autonomy to complete the work as they see fit.

Analyzing the Response

How to Get More Mileage Out of the Question. Candidates will readily admit if they are more inclined to inspect than to expect subordinates' work. The initial answer you get, however, is limited because it only superficially identifies the person's supervisory orientation. The key lies in unraveling the *degree* of inspection or expectation. For example, you might ask:

> "Dennis, you define yourself as someone who inspects his subordinates' work more than he expects good work from them. My next question for you is what is the average tenure of your sales team? Are these folks all new to the business, or are they fairly seasoned?"

When Dennis responds that he's got a fairly green sales team with one year of experience on average since college graduation, his inspection management style makes lots of sense. If, on the other hand, Dennis had a lot of senior account executives under his wing, then you'd have to wonder whether his overbearing style didn't detract from the team's potential. Yet a third query in this string would be, "Dennis, how successful is your team compared with other sales teams within your organization?" If his team ranks toward the back of the line because its members are young and inexperienced, then that inspection style again makes sense. Similarly, if his team of senior account executives ranks at the front of the polls, then his "inspection" style works, so don't mess with it.

Whatever the case, beware the ramifications of the individual's supervisory inclinations. If he's optimistic and altruistic by nature and expects his people to perform out of pure self-motivation, then his underperforming junior sales team may lack the proper discipline for success. If he's a taskmaster and his mature sales team shows only lackluster performance, then he may be riding them too hard and squelching creativity.

Ask, "Given the nature of your sales team, might it make more sense to inject a greater sense of [discipline/freedom] into their work environment? How would you do that, and how long would you expect it to take to see concrete results?" Such an invitation might just take the conversation into a new direction of self-admitted weaknesses, and that in turn could lead to honest introspection regarding a too harsh or too lenient supervisory approach.

30. How do you approach your work from the standpoint of balancing your career with your personal life?

Why Ask This Question?

This is an open invitation to engage in a person-to-person values session. No work-related accomplishments. No self-admitted weaknesses. No "What was the last time you had to bring bad news to your boss, and how did you handle it?" This is a purely human communication that transcends everything "businessy" about an interview. Although it borders on getting a little too personal for a typical business meeting, it does open the lines of communication by taking the interview to a deeper, more humanistic plane.

Analyzing the Response

Because of the lighter nature of this question, it typically won't turn into a knockout factor in the candidate selection process. However, because certain companies do expect employees to live for their organizations, this query might reveal certain expectations toward commitment that could hinder your relationship. For example, some companies expect their employees to come in to work before 7:30, leave after 8:00 at night, and come to work on Saturdays. A staunch reply from a candidate intimating that "My private time is not to be messed with" might cool off an otherwise hot interview.

In contrast, a self-proclaimed workaholic might leave you feeling ambivalent about an otherwise successful interview if you personally believe that work is a means to an end and that working to live is preferable to living to work. Again, in case you strongly espouse either theory or find yourself working in a company with stringent expectations regarding employee time commitments, then add this query to your arsenal to see whether any extreme emotions will surface that could eventually clash with your personal expectations or corporate culture.

31. Paint a picture of the corporate culture you'll create if we hire you. Do you operate under a more centralized and paternalistic agenda with power centralized in the hands of a few, or do you constantly push responsibility and accountability down the line?

Why Ask This Question?

You often hear of a "company's" corporate culture when in fact any given organization will have multiple cultures in different departments. The marketing manager may be well schooled in progressive human resource principals like empowerment, quality circles, and cross-functional teams. The manufacturing manager may have come from an environment where you're expected to do your job, say yes to your boss, and collect your paycheck. Trying to describe a single corporate culture in such a company would be well nigh impossible. Labeling the marketing or manufacturing unit's cultures, on the other hand, should be fairly easy to do. The bottom line, therefore, is that individual managers dictate the way a unit does business. You need to know a candidate's vision of how work will get done and how people will interact in order to avoid surprises down the road.

Analyzing the Response

How to Get More Mileage Out of the Question. If a candidate has trouble putting her hands around this question, you could follow up with a brief explanation to clarify what you want to learn:

> "Mary, what will life as we know it now turn into ninety days after we hire you? How will the work flow, how will people react to one another in your unit, how many weekly meetings will be going on, and how will our customers know that there's been a change?"

Obviously, the answers you get will be cast in the most positive light possible. Still, by requiring specific answers, you'll generate details regarding the candidate's personal style and expectations.

Let's take the case of Emma White, a candidate for informational technology (IT) manager at a plastics manufacturing organization outside of Springdale, Arkansas. She was applying for a position that would oversee a staff of ten programmer analysts, technical writers, and PC user support reps. Her mandate, if hired, would be to increase morale in a department with lots of tenure but very little enthusiasm for change, and within one year transition the department from an HP3000 to a Windows client-server environment.

Here's how Emma responded to the query:

"I like to hold a lot of meetings. It's important to me that everyone in my unit feels tied in to the bigger picture, and without that added element of human interaction, I find it difficult to bring a staff of people together in a coordinated effort. Not only do those meetings keep us all abreast of what's going on at a more global level, but they give the staff a chance to surface new and creative ideas to make operations run more smoothly. After all, a round table brainstorming session gets my creative juices up and running, and I've found that it works well for others too.

"In terms of increasing morale, those two or three roundtable meetings each week would make up step one of a plan designed to improve morale. I would also designate certain members of the department to lead meetings—depending on their areas of expertise—and depend on them to raise others' morale. Finally, I would propose holding companywide meetings to sell our IT services to the rest of the organization. For example, we could train company employees in word processing, spreadsheet, and e-mail skills. We'd cost out how much an outside service would charge for such training, and then we'd deliver those cost savings to senior management as part of our formal proposal to begin training.

"In the meantime, I would enroll my own staff in Windows client-server courses that would enhance their own technical skills, so that by the time we came to the conversion start date next year their confidence and competence would smooth the transition process. That plan should work to increase departmental morale; have spillover, morale-boosting effects for the rest of the company; and simultaneously ease our transition to the new software applications."

So how did Emma score? She made an excellent case for empowering her staff by pushing responsibility and accountability down the line. Her desire to tie staff members into the more global picture seems attainable because she'll get her IT people (a staff function) focused on profit and loss line considerations by having them cost out external training programs and then delivering a cost-benefit analysis. And her commitment to her staff's broader educational goals shows that she'll make good use of her first year on the job, because the planned transition to the client-server platform won't begin until her second year.

The response to this question can provide some valuable insights into a "new and improved" departmental corporate culture that may be very compatible with the company's style of doing business. And if the candidate's answer isn't compatible, then this detailed picture of "life ninety days into the job" should provide you with enough information to confirm that you want a different style of manager at the helm of your IT team.

Seven

The College Campus Recruit

Interviewing newly minted graduates has its own unique challenges because so little of their experience has any relevance to real life in the business world. That's not to say that these students haven't worked very hard to maintain a solid grade point average or to finance their educations. Nor does it in any way minimize the skills they've developed through team sports, fraternity leadership, or travel abroad. It's just that their university experiences don't easily lend themselves to measurable business criteria, and therein lies your challenge.

That being the case, many interviewers find themselves in the land of hypothetical questions. And hypothetical "What would you do if . . ." questioning formats reveal very little insight into how candidates will actually perform on the job. Indeed, if there is one area of interviewing that can be rehearsed and memorized, it's the hypothetical situation. That's because hypothetical questions test candidates' abilities only to theorize about their potential future performance. Also, candidates are given so much freedom to express themselves that their responses are prone to exaggeration.

So instead of asking candidates to hypothesize about life in the business world, you're better off meeting them at their level and asking behavioral questions regarding their reality: life on campus. For what you need to measure in the new graduate is the same as what you gauge in a timeworn business person: the quality of the person's character. After all, any new hire is simply a bet that you make in terms of the individual's potential to give your company a competitive advantage someday. That's why you can justify the fact that you'll most likely take a loss in the new hires' first year while you're putting all that training into them.

Still, characteristics like common sense, tenacity, reliability, and leadership go a long way in making your company a more successful operation. And everyone's got to start somewhere, so targeting eager and hungry graduates ready to make their mark on the world may make sense for you. You've just got to be sure of two things: first, that candidates are somewhat aware of what they want in life (otherwise, your company becomes one of the frogs that need to be kissed before they find their prince); second, that graduates' strengths can readily be translated from an academic to a business context. Following are some questions that should help make more accurate assessments of recent graduates' abilities to make a solid impact on your company over time.

32. Why did you choose your [*college/major*]?

Why Ask This Question?

Let's be practical about this. Most larger universities probably offer close to one hundred majors from which to choose. The four with the most direct real-life practical application are engineering, pre-med, computer science, and business. Does that mean that those economics, German, anthropology, kinesiology, and geography majors have little to offer? Of course not. As a matter of fact, study after study has been published regarding which students fare better in business: those with liberal arts orientations or those with specialty degrees. Keep in mind, however, that unless you're hiring for one of the Big 6 accounting firms, you'll have about a 95 percent chance of interviewing students with majors that have little relevance to your direct line of business. So employing this query will allow you to tunnel inside their heads for a moment and gauge what interests them and why.

Analyzing the Response

This is obviously an opening query to get the candidate talking freely. It's no doubt the most often asked question in the on-campus interview, but it serves its purpose because it puts candidates at ease while providing you with a framework from which to judge the rest of their responses. Bear in mind as well that 80 percent of the hire is determined in the first few minutes of the interview. That means that candidates with clearly defined responses to such a "macro" issue will place themselves at the top of the pile right from the git-go. Your key in evaluating the response will look for career managers and career builders in the making.

Good Answers. For example, if someone chooses a university because it has one of the best academic programs in that individual's major field of study, then there is a strong chance that the candidate had her eye on that college while still in high school. If so, you might question,

"What did you have to achieve in high school to make the final cut to get into this university?" Such long-term insights on the candidate's part reveal a commitment to project completion and a high tolerance for adversity. In short, this person reaches the goals she sets for herself.

Furthermore, if a candidate chooses an economics major because he feels that the lateral thinking skills developed in those studies would prepare him better for studying law, then similarly view that person as a long-term career builder who will most likely finish what he starts. What about the German major who wants a chance to study abroad and understand the psychology of a people by studying their literature and poetry as opposed to their history and politics? Ditto! Does it matter whether the economics major decided against law school or the German major against a career in foreign diplomacy? Of course not. The point is that these students reveal a quality of character difficult to find nowadays: a premeditated devotion and an unceasing follow-up to academic areas that mean a lot to them. Look for these "macro" visionaries ten years later, and you'll find leaders in all fields of business.

33. How does your degree prepare you (a) for a career in [*industry*] or (b) to excel as a [*job title*]?

Why Ask This Question?

Moving deductively from the generic to the specific, this query asks candidates to make a causal connection between their academic majors and their targeted first positions out of college. It will not only justify why the candidates have chosen to interview with your firm, but it may provide insights into graduates' inclinations to research a situation before committing to it.

For example, before conducting on-campus interviews, you would typically forward your annual report and public relations materials to the university placement center. Candidates who research your organization in advance and ask questions related to your organization's market niche, short-term challenges, or the outside influences that have a direct impact on your business operations clearly separate themselves from their peers. And since most universities offer on-line Internet services, even if you haven't provided your company's annual report in advance, there's little excuse for a graduating senior—even in the midst of finals—not to have taken ten minutes to learn what Wall Street Research Net (http://www.wsrn.com) or Hoovers (http:www.hoovers.com) or America On Line's "Edgar" system has to say about your firm.

Analyzing the Response

How to Get More Mileage Out of the Question. Asking graduates "How has your degree prepared you for a career in advertising?" or "How has your degree prepared you to excel as a staff accountant at our Big 6 accounting firm?" should reveal the link in the candidate's career progression from academia to business. Here again, you'll be faced with something of a jump in imagination as candidates relate their theoretical learnings to real-life future performance. Your challenge will lie in equating excellence in general skill categories with specific functions back at the office.

For example, a graduate who worked as a research assistant is probably inquisitive and resourceful enough to handle a position that requires investigative skills. Similarly, someone who writes for the school paper reveals a creative bent. Editors of that same school paper are probably more inclined to analysis. And student tutors probably have more of a knack for public speaking and customer service. There's no absolute matrix that will clearly place certain college-related activities into a business context, but translating from academia to business isn't a cut-and-dried science. That's why interviews are in essence opinions about an individual's ability to provide you with a profitable return on investment over time. And that's also what makes the evaluation process fun and challenging!

34. What qualifications do you have beyond academics that qualify you to make a successful transition into business?

Why Ask This Question?

Students with a broad base of extracurricular activities and community involvement show a high capacity for dealing with changing priorities and balancing multiple tasks. That's not to say that students who do little beyond their expected course work can't perform as well in an environment with last-minute changes and competing demands. As a matter of fact, the competition among pre-med students is so intense that one tenth of a point's difference on their grade point average could determine which graduate schools accept or reject them. So if you're hiring doctors, then you'll probably value academic genius above all else.

Still, most businesses require well-rounded individuals with lots to give in terms of networking with other businesspeople, attending industry-related functions, and finding time to make a presence in the community. Therefore, extracurricular activities say a lot about graduates' inclinations to make broad-based contributions to multiple organizations.

Analyzing the Response

Only you can determine how much extracurricular activity is enough as far as your organizational hiring profile is concerned. And only you can discern what grade point average will suffice to predict success in your company. But there obviously has to be a practical trade-off between the number of nonacademic activities and candidates' final grade point averages because they can't be studying when marching around the football field playing the trumpet or working in the neighborhood grocery store thirty hours a week to finance their educations.

Extracurricular qualifications consequently come in two varieties: (1) school-related and community-based activities and (2) working arrangements to finance an education. Both are noble in terms of their broadening the depth of students' appreciation and heightening the whole experience of advanced learning. Additionally, some crucial issues may surface that provide clearer insights into the candidate evaluation process.

Those students who participate in the same school-related activities for all four years reveal a level of commitment and discipline that is not easily shaken. The continuity in their actions also shows that they have fairly well come to terms with their strengths and interests and pursue them steadfastly. Others explore multiple activities and disciplines before (if ever) committing to one that can apparently hold their interest. Again, there's nothing wrong with that; not everyone will be a four-year letterman on the football team.

RED FLAGS. But it is interesting to see how diverse and eclectic those students' elective activities turn out. For example, someone who's tried everything from swim team to chess club to sorority membership may appear somewhat flighty and inconsistent. If you notice that each of those memberships lasted no more than a semester, then you might logically reason that the individual has difficulty committing to longer-term organizational relationships. Whether that's enough to ultimately serve as a negative swing factor is up to you. The inconsistency, however, is telling.

How to Get More Mileage Out of the Question. In comparison, students who work flipping hamburgers, waiting tables, or tutoring other students will most likely appreciate the value of their educations from a dollars-and-cents standpoint. These are the self-made, independent types who typically rely on no one other than themselves for their success or failure. What they lack in terms of "enriching" extracurricular experiences they make up for in a heightened sense of self-reliance and self-determination. Accordingly, you might question:

> "What particular business skills did you develop while working your way through college?"

> "How might you have an advantage over a peer who was enjoying fraternity life and other 'fun' activities while you were employed in a less than glamorous job?"

> "How could the adversity you faced from the pressure of meeting your financial obligations affect your work ethic and approach to business?"

In short, look for the skills, values, and work ethic developed from hard labor. As they say, hard work never killed anybody. Combined with the pressures of meeting demanding academic performance standards, such a rigorous agenda of activities portends a particularly successful transition into business.

35. Do you think your grades are a good indicator of your ability to succeed in business?

Why Ask This Question?

Ah, tough question! But it certainly gets right to the heart of the matter. After all, every interview deserves its challenging moments. As a matter of fact, some employers choose to really lay on the pressure with queries such as "Why are your grades so erratic? Why didn't you get better grades? Did you really think that a psychology major would qualify you to land a job in company like ours?" and the like. These pressure cookers, however, can unnerve even the most self-confident candidates. Unless you're looking for someone who can really take rejection and deal in a boiler-room environment, you're better off leaving these nasty questions out of your interviewing agenda. They build little goodwill and test nothing other than the candidate's ability to tell you what you want to hear.

Analyzing the Response

Are grades in and of themselves clear indicators of potential job performance? To answer that, think about your own career experience. If you were clearly a C student and now rank within the top fifth percentile of sales producers in your company, then your need to locate a straight-A student will probably be negligible. If, on the other hand, you were a straight-A student and made a stellar transition into an insurance company as an actuary, then you might logically reason that academic grades necessarily correlate to logical thought patterns and self-imposed discipline.

RED FLAGS. The point is that most people hire in their own image. Grades, consequently, may reflect an individual's potential performance, but that's not guaranteed. What's more important in the interview process, though, is how the student feels about the correlation between grades and work potential. If the candidate immediately begins to apologize for less-than-stellar grades, beware: you might end up with someone lacking self-esteem and confidence in his abilities. On the other hand, if the individual fails to come to terms with his flagging academic performance, then you may be faced with a graduate who fails to assume responsibility for his actions and who bends the truth to subjectively paint pictures in his favor.

What's the ideal answer? An open admission of the individual's shortcomings. Few graduates sport straight-A grades. For example, consider someone who responds like this:

> "I was a B- student and took five years to complete my degree, but I worked thirty hours a week to finance my education, and I was the first in my family to attend college. I'm proud of my performance and did the best I could with the time and resources available to me."

This individual accepts her shortcomings and reveals a healthy ego. Similarly, a response like the following accounts for what the student was doing when not studying:

> "I had a C average as an English major, but I was awarded the Freshman of the Year Award in the marching band and served my fraternity as president in my senior year."

There's a very healthy trade-off between time at study and time holding leadership roles on campus, so that balance atones for a less-than-perfect grade point average.

By contrast, beware the student who blames others for her failures. A nagging and complaining tone like, "Well, I could've had better grades if I didn't have to work all the time" or "My 2.5 GPA corresponds to a 3.5 GPA if I hadn't participated in so many community-based activities and had as much time to study as everyone else" portends poor performance. After all, no one needs to apologize for less-than-perfect grades. More importantly, no one should blame others for circumstances beyond her control. That's a trait that definitely translates from academia to business, and it's a headache that you need to avoid.

36. What other types of positions and companies are you considering right now?

Why Ask This Question?

This question helps you accurately assess what kind of expectations a graduate has for himself. If those plans are realistic and logically tie into what your organization has to offer, then there's an excellent chance that you won't be one of those frogs that many recent grads have to kiss before they find their prince. If the individual's plans are too casual or undeveloped, on the other hand, there may be a serious lack of commitment to starting a business career.

Analyzing the Response

Whenever possible, most college grads will attempt to find a position that ties into their majors. Foreign language majors apply to the diplomacy schools to ultimately become ambassadors to the United Nations; film majors send their resumés to the major Hollywood studios; physical education majors contact all the major football, basketball, and baseball franchises; and physical anthropology majors apply to become docents at the nearest museum of natural history. So what should it tell you when a film major is applying with your plastics manufacturing organization for an entry-level sales position? Probably that the heavens are out of sync and the individual isn't totally dedicated to making your company a life-long pursuit!

How to Get More Mileage Out of the Question. To gather more data, ask questions like these:

> "Mary, you were a film major. If you could rub on a magic lamp and apply your studies directly to the working world, what would you ideally be doing? Why are you interviewing for positions other than those in the film world? How long would you realistically expect it to take to land your first job in the film industry, and what will you do in the meantime while you're waiting for your first break?"

Your assumption in this situation is clear to the candidate: Why aren't you seeking to use immediately the knowledge and skills you worked so hard to gain over the past four years?

Your assumption to yourself will be equally lucid: "There's some reason why this person isn't looking for a job in the film business. I've got to find out, though, before I tempt fate and bring her aboard." You are entitled, after all, to continuity in the positions you fill. If a candidate wants to get her feet wet in the business world, she should temp for while rather than accept a full-time position with a half-hearted commitment.

Next, it's critical that you gauge the caliber of companies and industries that the candidate is pursuing in addition to your opportunity. If all the positions are in the financial services arena in some capacity related to customer service, then you're safe in assuming that the individual's consistency reveals her true desires. If the candidate is interviewing "all over the map" with meetings set up for retail positions, office administrative work, and product manufacturing, then she probably lacks direction.

Having eclectic tastes and an inquisitive, experimental nature can be a virtue in certain circumstances, but it's a disadvantage when searching for a first job. Simply ask the candidate:

> "Doris, I see that you're exploring very diverse opportunities. What criteria are you using in selecting your career path? How would you rank the various opportunities in terms of your interest level?"

Forcing the situation could cause the candidate some discomfort, but it will help clarify for you exactly where your opportunity stands in her pecking order. And that will help ensure that the bet you're making regarding this individual's potential minimizes the downside risk that she'll be gone before you've had a chance to recoup your investment in training.

College campus interviewing is one of the most exhilarating areas of career evaluation because of the candidates' excitement and eagerness to open a new chapter in their lives and to make a contribution that will lead to serious income and independence. Evaluating candidates correctly will help you learn which ones are apt to influence your company most positively. Your skilled questioning techniques will also serve to teach them more about themselves—their desires, strengths, limitations, and motivations—on their way to new career paths.

Eight

Profiling Secretaries and Administrative Support Staff: The People Who Really Make Your Organization Work!

Little need be said of an excellent secretary's impact on the boss's performance. The advent of the PC in the early 1980s changed forever the way companies do business, and the secretarial function benefited greatly in terms of increased accountability and opportunities for self-expression. That's because the computer bridged the information gap between senior-level decision makers and operative employees. The middle manager's role as purveyor of information across traditional corporate boundaries was drastically reduced, causing an unprecedented white-collar recession in the early 1990s. Accordingly, cost-conscious companies in a competitive global economy learned how to simultaneously decrease payrolls and increase productivity per employee.

The secretarial-executive relationship has since become a key power-partner alliance at the top level of corporate America. That's because secretaries are very closely linked to the information flow generated by the PC and are capable of exploiting its applications. As executives became more dependent on their assistants to reconfigure information into databases, spreadsheets, and graphics presentations, those secretaries assumed new roles as researcher, ghostwriter, and discretionary confidant. Gone forever was the paradigm of the clerical "gopher" banging out documents in typing pools. Here to stay is the empowered assistant capable of dealing effectively with all levels of management, producing correspondence with pinpoint contextual and grammatical accuracy, and maintaining a smooth work flow in the boss's absence.

The following interview queries will gauge a candidate's work style, technical expertise, and tolerance for dealing with adversity. These questions typically work well for all levels of administrative support employees from clerks and receptionists to high-powered administrative assistants. They tend to be more personal and subjective in nature than other questions we've examined in this book because a successful outcome in hiring support staff—more so than any other type of new hire in corporate America—directly links itself to compatible work styles and personal preferences between supervisor and subordinate.

Remember again that the following five questions are not the only queries that you'll want to use in an interview. Other topics throughout this book offer excellent ideas to help gather critical information. Still, these five questions crystallize some of the key issues necessary in hiring administrative support staff, so put them to work for you in your next interview!

37. How would you grade your ability to predict needs before they arise? In other words, how would you evaluate your intuition, timeliness, and proactive business style?

Why Ask This Question?

Probably the most critical talent for anyone in an assistant role is to head off problems at the pass—to keep two steps ahead of every project so that snags are avoided and deadlines are met. Such organizational forecasting ability ensures a smooth work flow and protects your flank, so to speak, as you speedily pass off work to your assistant without worry that it will be completed accurately.

Analyzing the Response

How to Get More Mileage Out of the Question. In applying this question during the interview, you need once again to employ a behavioral interviewing format to add dimension to the individual's response. Qualify the candidate's initial response with a follow-up like: "Give me an example of the last time your boss commended you for staying on top of the workload and bringing a project to a smooth completion." On the other hand, you could look for contrary evidence by questioning, "Tell me about an experience you had in which you miscalculated which way the work was heading. How did you recoup and get back on track?"

For example, a corporate travel coordinator might respond to this initial question this way:

> "I believe that I am good at predicting needs and problems before they arise. For example, I accepted a newly created position at my last company and was mandated to set up an infrastructure to coordinate corporate travel. The organization had a $250,000 travel budget, but surprisingly, there weren't any specified rules regarding hotel expense reimbursements, ground transportation guidelines, or even a list of preapproved hotels with direct billing accounts. I could see the confusion that might arise from this nebulous situation. Within three months, I created a very efficient system for handling corporate travel, including the selection of a new national travel agency to generate budget and expense reports."

To flesh out the candidate's response, you can ask:

> "That sounds like a big job, Mary Jo. Give me an example of the first thing you did when presented with that overwhelming problem. How did you organize your game plan?"

> "Tell me about the first time you hit a major snag. Was it an internal problem related, perhaps, to additional expenses you needed, or was it an external issue where vendors were reluctant to meet your needs?"

> "At the end of that third month when the system was in place, what was your boss's response? How did she recognize your achievement in creating a corporate travel infrastructure and your timeliness in meeting your goals?"

Setting up a travel system is a great accomplishment, but if the boss isn't adequately praising the employee's achievement, perhaps it's because the time it took to create the plan was way out of line with expected timetables. Or perhaps the draconian measures that Mary Jo took to reach her goals angered everyone she had to deal with in the process. The bottom line is that behavioral questions can provide you with more accurate outcomes hiding just below the surface once the specific details shade in the response.

38. Do you consider your technical abilities basic, intermediate, or advanced? What types of projects did you complete with each software program?

Why Ask This Question?

If the premise entering into this chapter is that secretaries and other administrative support staff workers have witnessed a tremendous opportunity for job enrichment since the advent of the PC, then those individuals' technical skills are commensurate with their abilities to make a positive impact on your organization. Not every candidate needs to be a Windows guru or a World Wide Web surfer gliding along the Internet. Still, technical literacy is the sine qua non in the world of administrative support. Only you can determine just how much PC power you need in an assistant. If your firm doesn't use PC literacy testing software in the candidate evaluation process (and it probably won't unless your company hires large volumes of these types of workers fairly frequently), then you should by all means address this essential job qualification during your meeting.

Analyzing the Response

Most administrative support candidates have a basic mastery of (1) word processors, (2) spreadsheets, (3) relational databases, (4) graphics software packages, and possibly (5) the Internet. Of course, the computer industry is the fastest-changing market the world has ever seen. It's estimated that the information supply available doubles every five years, and programs upgrade constantly. So what's in one year may quickly be out the next. Still, there's one trap that many employers fall into, and that's got to be addressed right now.

Many employers mistakenly equate typing speed with employee productivity. Typing speed used to be an objective assessment tool to compare different candidates' potential output on an even playing field. Back in the days of secretarial pools producing typewritten documents, that was an accurate measure. Today, however, the key to evaluating technical skills lies in measuring computer savvy, not typing speed. The strongest administrative assistants are able to electronically revamp their bosses' schedules and efficiently automate their environment. Personal information managers, file managers, and other types of software have exploded on the retail sales shelf and, in the right assistant's hands, can dramatically affect the boss's life. Typing speed in and of itself consequently takes on a far less critical role than it did before, so don't give the issue undue focus in the selection process.

How to Get More Mileage Out of the Question. In querying candidates regarding their technical competency levels, remember that self-

evaluation terms like "basic, intermediate, or advanced" are totally arbitrary. You will therefore have to ask the candidate: "Ted, you say your
word processing skills are basic. What does 'basic' mean to you? What
kind of functions would a word processor with basic skills be able to do?"

Furthermore, to flesh out the candidate's definition more accurately,
ask, "How technically oriented are you compared to your peers?" and
"How fluent are you at simultaneously linking together information from
word processors, spreadsheets, and databases into master documents?"
You'll immediately gain an understanding of the individual's familiarity
with cross-functional PC skills (if you require that). You'll also develop a
much clearer picture of a candidate's ability to help you create computer-
generated slides for your next presentation, tap the Internet to recruit for
a current job opening in your department, or produce mail merges to
keep your clients abreast of your newest business development programs.

39. In what areas do you typically have the least amount of patience at work?

Why Ask This Question?

This very personal question belongs in this chapter because few relationships are as intimate as the executive-assistant alliance. Finding compatible business styles is critical to the selection process because not only
do your strengths and inclinations need to match each other, but your
individual shortcomings need to be openly discussed as well.

Analyzing the Response

Good Answers. You'll typically find that candidates will shy away
from addressing situations that try their patience because there is simply
nothing to gain by offering a truthful response. They're supposed to be
patient with their bosses, customers, and subordinates all the time. Period. Many interviewees will speak solely about their impatience with
their own performance, thereby avoiding placing blame on anyone else.
That's an acceptable response. After all, it is often said that so long as we
search beyond ourselves for solutions, we disempower ourselves. Finally,
others will raise acceptable issues regarding their impatience with coworkers who feel entitled to a job or entitled to job security just because
they show up at work every day. This is also a very legitimate response.

How to Get More Mileage Out of the Question. The most effective way to apply this subjective and emotional query is to follow up the candidate's initial response with other questions that add a concrete context. Asking two or three questions like these will yield a more realistic image of what the daily work environment will be like:

"What is it like working with you? What should I expect on a day-to-day basis?"

"How much structure should I be prepared to give you? Do you like lots of feedback and direction, or would you prefer that I left you alone once I established what needed to be done?"

"How do you expect me to delegate work to you? Will you come to me asking for more work, or will you expect me to come to you to see if you're ready to assume additional responsibilities?"

"How do you plan to keep me 'in the loop' in terms of what's going on at your desk? Could I expect constant feedback, or should I meet with you throughout the day to follow up on where you are?"

"Project for me what your ninety-day performance evaluation will look like. What will be your strengths, and what will be your weaknesses?"

You might not like working with someone who needs lots of structure and direction in his day or someone who waits to have work handed to him. You might need someone to casually keep you in the information loop rather than formally meet with you at periodic intervals. Or you might opt for an assistant who pulls files off your desk rather than waits for you to hand them over. Most managers don't learn about these stylistic issues until well after the candidate has already begun work. By adding such emotional queries to your initial evaluation, you'll be in much better shape to match a candidate's style of doing business to your own.

40. How would you grade your ability to communicate with upper-level management, customers, and peers?

Why Ask This Question?

Career experts rank communication skills as the highest priority in a successful business career. However, cultural and personality differences exist that reveal themselves in varying levels of persistence, aggressiveness, stamina, and stubbornness. These issues could be further assessed during a reference check while speaking with a candidate's former employer. Still, questioning the individual about her own personality assessment can reveal whether or not she is in sync with your corporate culture and management style.

Analyzing the Response

How to Get More Mileage Out of the Question. A typical candidate response will sound fairly benign and lack the concrete details necessary for you to truly gauge the person's communication skills: "I get along well with others, and I'm very well liked and respected by my peers" is a common comeback. True, this is a tougher question. Few people, after all, will voluntarily admit that they're too aggressive in pursuing their own agendas, too quiet and shy to stand up for themselves, or too inclined to maintain smooth and amicable relations at all costs. Your job, consequently, will be to add some concrete critical mass to this issue by questioning:

"Tell me about the last time you became 'unwound' while dealing with coworkers. What tried your patience or caused your anger?"

"Have you ever found it necessary to show your teeth, so to speak, and not back down in a confrontation with a peer, customer, or superior?"

"Give me an example of the most irrational, rude, and intimidating customer you had to deal with at your last position. How did you handle the situation? In retrospect, how could you have handled it differently? How did your boss grade your performance?"

"Would coworkers say that you're more casual and relaxed or more intense and focused?"

"Tell me about the last time you chose to bring to your boss's attention something she did that hurt your feelings or took you for granted. Do you openly discuss those kinds of issues as soon as they occur? Do you hold them in until you're ready to burst? Are you emotionally charged in those kinds of meetings, or do you find that you're totally calm and rational?"

Detailing very specific situations forces individuals to replay memorable sound bytes by which they identify themselves. Those insights will help paint accurate pictures of what the "business marriage" will look like once the honeymoon's over.

41. What pace do you typically work at?

Why Ask This Question?

If you define your company as a high-velocity operation, finding people to keep up with you could be more than challenging. If, on the other hand, your corporate culture adheres to a more relaxed and loose standard, then avoiding high-strung workaholics may be your safest bet. When pace and speed are a particular concern, then raise this issue to determine compatibility.

Analyzing the Response

Most people will respond to this query by saying, "Oh, I definitely work at and prefer a fast pace with lots of variety." Of course, such generic responses beg you to dive into your behavioral interviewing bag of tricks and ask the candidate to describe a typical work situation centering around the pace of the office: "Tell me how you define 'fast pace' and 'variety.' What is it about you that makes you operate at that speed?" You might then look for contrary evidence probing for times when the candidate might have been considered too slow in getting something done or a situation when a deadline was missed: "Give me an example of a time when you missed a deadline. How did the pace of the office outrun you, and what did you do regroup and fix the problem?"

How to Get More Mileage Out of the Question. Yet another way to clarify this issue during the interview is to define your idea of "pace" more clearly for the candidate. It might sound something like this:

"Barbara, you say that you like a fast pace with lots of variety. Let me ask a more specific question. If you had to choose among three speeds that define your work style most accurately, would you want:

1. A more moderate, controllable, and predictable environment,
2. A faster-paced atmosphere with deadline pressures and time constraints, or

3. A hyperspace, chaotic, management-by-crisis culture like that on the trading floor of a stock exchange?"

In clearly delineating the various kinds of paces to be found in an office, you'll reveal the candidates' comfort zones quickly. Those who choose option 1 typically are either perfectionists and "controllers" (in the sense that they have to tie all loose ends together in the first project before moving on to the second project) or they're people who aren't looking for a lot of extra pressure. In the latter case, those people often want a job, but not necessarily a career. And that's not altogether bad—many jobs require people to handle repetitive tasks, and hiring a career climber for that type of role could quickly lead to premature turnover.

People who choose option 3 live their lives at lightning speed. They tend to be high-volume producers simply by the fact that more information passes through their desks than that of an average worker. (Of course, high volume may be adversely proportionate to quality, but there are other questions to tackle the quality issue.) More importantly, these people often have the ability to cope with a work life that is going to be "fuzzy around the edges." Accordingly, they fare better in an environment with lots of balls in the air where project completion jumps from assignment 1 to assignment 5 and then back to 3.

Most candidates who are asked this question respond that they prefer option 2: a faster-paced environment with deadline pressures and time constraints. The reason for this is that moderate and predictable environments sound lackluster; "flying by the seat of your pants" chaotic environments sound too stressful; deadline pressures and time constraints, on the other hand, typically keep people focused and appear to offer variety—a very desirable perk for many administrative support folks.

These interview questions should go a long way in getting candidates to articulate detailed anecdotes about their past successes and failures as well as their ability to manage change and land on their feet. No set of finite questions will work in every hiring scenario: Your needs as an employer will change over time as turnover occurs in your ranks. Still, questions that help candidates subjectively assess themselves will maximize the chances of making this "emotional" superior-subordinate relationship work over the long run. It's worth repeating that few other relationships in your company will be as dependent upon a personal style match as this one.

Nine

The Sales Interview: Differentiating Among Top Producers, Rebel Producers, and Those Who Struggle to the Minimums

No doubt about it: The sales interview is typically one of the most challenging evaluations you'll encounter, with a hefty impact on your organization's bottom line. That's because top producers often march to their own drummers. Some focus on quantity of transactions, while others build relationships over the long haul. Some consistently produce in the stratosphere, while others merely earn enough to get by. Some have more of a nine-to-five mindset than an entrepreneurial mentality and consequently rarely perform with distinction. Still others unfortunately define success not in terms of their accomplishments, but by their peers' failures. Although such "rebel producers" often close the month at the top of the charts, they pull down the production of their team members in the process.

So how do you determine the potential of the stockbroker or loan officer or computer sales representative sitting in front of you? Equally important, how do you anticipate the impact that this individual will have in terms of complementing your existing staff? Bear in mind that your task will be made "fuzzier" by the fact that salespeople are skilled at saying all the right things and landing on their feet in "cold call" situations—which is exactly what your interview represents to them. In addition, many salespeople are criticized for selling their business better than doing their business. That means that many of them will sell themselves better than they'll actually perform on the job. So where does that leave you—the line manager with ultimate say over who gets to play on the team?

Because there are no clear-cut questions and answers that assess sales professionals consistently, you'll have to employ a series of questions that will help paint a picture of the individual's manner of doing business . . . a group of questions that, taken together, will address drive, energy, impulsiveness, discipline, and commitment. Patterns and inconsistencies will emerge only when these topics are addressed from several different angles.

42. How do you competitively rank among other account executives in terms of your production?

Why Ask This Question?

Salespeople are typically bottom-line types who relish the chase of closing a deal and who measure themselves via their peer ranking. Opening your interview with a bottom-line question regarding the individual's production sets the tone for the rest of the meeting. Those with the most to offer will challenge you to provide them with even greater responsibilities. The opportunities they're looking for will come in the form of stronger commission payouts or long-term management opportunities.

In comparison, those who haven't been able to attain consistent sales often change jobs because they're not making enough money. Excuses and apologies drive candidates from company to company searching for illusory payout packages that will earn them higher wages. The reason why they're not more successful, however, is typically found in their inability to establish rapport, identify a prospect's needs, distinguish features from benefits, overcome objections, or most importantly, close the deal. Your mission, consequently, will be to locate each individual's shortcomings.

Analyzing the Response

Good Answers. In response to this question, candidates often rank themselves according to percentages and quartiles:

"I rank among the leading 10 percent of auto sales executives in my region."

"My numbers are typically in the top 25th percentile of stock-brokers in my firm."

"I received a President's Club award for finishing last year as the number 4 producer companywide."

"My production typically placed me in the lower 50th percentile in terms of sales, but that's because. . . ."

Obviously those who enjoy the distinguished reputation of ranking at the top have no difficulty sharing those achievements with you. Sales is all about competition, and those who perform with distinction relish their positions of power. In such cases, most of your interview will be spent discussing how the top producer got there, stays there, and plans to obtain the next rung on the success ladder.

RED FLAGS. The last example, however, points to the problem producer. Salespeople who do not reach acceptable performance benchmarks immediately volunteer reasons why their numbers were not higher. Sometimes excuses are acceptable; other times they have very little credibility. Only you know what separates excellence from mediocrity in your field. Your primary focus, however, in dealing with individuals who rank themselves at the bottom of the heap lies in identifying the patterns for their excuses. Short-term tenures with similar types of companies usually spell inconsistent performance. In such instances, this interview question will immediately raise red flags in your mind. Proceed with caution, and measure the answers that follow in this light.

43. What are the two most common objections you face, and how do you deal with them?

Why Ask This Question?

Role-playing maintains a critical role in the sales interview. Because there are typically no more than two or three major objections that any account executive faces, it's important to hear how the candidate rebuts common rejections. This is an opportunity for the two of you to match wits. Hence, this role-play will provide you with insights into the individual's sophistication and creativity as the two of you measure each other up.

Analyzing the Response

What are the most typical objections in your industry? Here are some common ones:

"We don't have any needs for your product."

"We're happy with our current provider."

"We've got a long list of vendors who have already sent in sales materials. If you'd like to add your public relations material to our list, then when we open up for bids next January, we'll consider your proposal."

RED FLAGS. No matter what field of sales you're in, these stonewalling showstoppers typically throw salespeople off. So the first thing you want to observe is how confidently the candidate attacks the objection. Persuasion plays a big role, after all, in establishing rapport with new accounts. The second issue lies in the creativity of the individual's response: if her rebuttals sound like everyone else's in town, there's a chance that she hasn't given much thought to what makes her product or service unique.

Therefore, beware of candidates who regurgitate hackneyed responses like: "Well, what would you do if you suddenly needed a . . . ," "I bet we could offer more competitive rates than your current provider . . . ," or "Change is good. I'm sure that's how you found your current vendor in the first place. Why not give me a chance to show you what I could do?" Such trite and overused comebacks typically result in very little new business.

Good Answers. Look for responses, instead, that reveal creative insights and go beyond the obvious. For example, a stockbroker who possesses a CPA license might respond to an objection like "I've been working with my current broker for fourteen years" with this rebuttal:

"Nancy, I respect the relationship you have with your current provider. My only suggestion to you is that I might be able to provide you with financial advice under certain circumstances where your current broker can't. I'm a CPA, and my niche in the investment field is to help clients plan their portfolios with an eye toward the tax ramifications of fairly complex investment setups. I wouldn't expect you to jettison a personal relationship that you have with a friend just because I happened to phone you today. But I'd like your permission to send you information about my practice since I go where most brokers fear to tread. A number of attorneys depend on me to provide them with timely tax and estate planning advice, and I've been successful at tying that back-end knowledge into front-end investing. Does that sound like something that could eventually benefit you?"

Similarly, a copier salesperson might respond to the objection "I have no plans to purchase new machinery" like this:

"Doris, copiers and fax machines are only the products I sell, not the reason why I'm in business. I think that any vendor worth his salt will try to establish long-term relationships with as many companies as possible. The way I do that is by offering value-added service to people who need help when they're in a pinch. If your systems go down and your current provider is unavailable, call me. I'll be happy to personally walk you through the problem and find quick and practical solutions. Hopefully, if enough of a rapport is established over time, when you need to purchase new machinery, you'll naturally think of me. I know that doesn't sound like the way most copier sales-people develop business, but it's worked exceptionally well for me. I'd like to leave you my name and number in case I could ever be of service."

What's common to these responses? Creativity and uniqueness! People who leverage their backgrounds or education to a customer's advantage maintain an edge in the client development arena. Similarly, those who put the customer before the sale build goodwill and credibility. After all, not many stockbrokers hold CPA status. Most salespeople, as a matter of fact, do very little to understand what their clients do. So when an executive recruiter, for example, gets a certificate in human resources management in order to learn his clients' business, he'll stand out. Look for such commitment to the industry being serviced.

Salespeople who present their services on a problem-to-solution level and who show patience and goodwill in the sales process turn prospects on. There's no sales pitch and, even more importantly, the salesperson shows a commitment to building long-term relationships. Sophisticated, relationship-driven salespeople will consistently outperform transaction-driven, "buckshot" types who see no farther than this month's billing log.

How to Get More Mileage Out of the Question. Once you've gotten a rebuttal, pose a follow-up query as if you were the customer. Does the candidate respond to questions at face value, or does she try to close each response by setting an appointment? How many questions will she field before gaining some type of commitment from you? How does she respond to your requests for unreasonable discounts or service? On-the-spot role-plays, like pictures, paint a thousand words. Use them to gain valuable insights into the individual's style, character, and business savvy.

44. Role-play with me, if you will, presenting yourself to me over the phone as if you were a headhunter. Convince me that this "product" you're selling is worth my time.

Why Ask This Question?

No, this isn't only an exercise for hiring potential recruiters! Instead it is an exercise to replace a hackneyed and trite interviewing query used way too often in corporate America: "Sell me the pen." The problem with the "sell me the pen" scenario is that it's so overused that candidates come to expect it. That being the case, they prepare themselves to sell pens better than they sell their actual products!

The reason why this query has stood the test of time is because it forces job candidates to distinguish between the object's features and benefits; to overcome any objections that you, the pretend prospective buyer, could raise; and, most importantly, to "close" you on the purchase. However, Question 44 does all this much more effectively without being so predictable, so let's take a look at it.

Analyzing the Response

Asking candidates to sell themselves to you is challenging because they have to be totally objective about a very personal topic . . . namely, themselves! Distinguishing features from benefits isn't so easy when discussing their own strengths and limitations as well as what makes them stand out among their peers. Furthermore, because of the intimacy of the subject, most candidates are doubly challenged in providing role-play answers that mesh well with their interview responses. That added dimension of accountability often adds some circumspection to candidates' otherwise bold responses and makes overcoming objections and closing you on the hire a tougher challenge.

How to Get More Mileage Out of the Question. In evaluating candidates' responses, expect some initial discomfort. After all, no matter how confident candidates are, this exercise does set them up to brag about themselves. (And most people on a job interview don't want to go too overboard in that area.) Next, gauge the presentation. Does the individual start off the sales presentation timidly with a trite "How are you today?" or does the person get to the point right away? A creative presentation, for example, might sound like this:

> "Ms. Employer, I'm calling to tell you about a copier sales executive who's expressed an interest in meeting with your company because he's aware of your reputation, he works for a direct competitor, and he's thoroughly researched your organization. He ranks among the top 20 percent of producers in his company and has a proven track record of taking a poorly performing territory and increasing market share above the national average within two years. Would you consider talking to someone like that?"

Good Answers. It won't always sound this smooth, but the presentation should at least offer tangible results and future benefits. You're then free to lob some objections at the individual, including, "I have no openings," "Tell me more about him," and "What's he looking for?" After presenting an objection like "We have no openings," look for candidate rebuttals like, "Well, you know, Ms. Employer, it's been my experience that strong companies would set up an office in a closet for someone who could immediately add to their top-line revenues. Perhaps you'd consider comparing his track record to some of your existing staff." Such heads-up rebuttals show a great deal of ingenuity, creativity, and wit.

Finally, the "close" in this scenario lies in setting up the interview. See how aggressive the individual overcomes your objections and gets you to commit to meeting with a top producer if only on an exploratory basis. It's an exercise that will shed lots of light into candidates' self-esteem levels and their abilities to present a product that they're not naturally inclined to sell.

45. How do you define your closing style?

Why Ask This Question?

If there's one area in sales where people fail, it's in their inability to persuade a prospect to take a recommended course of action. Some people just never seem to master this one technique regardless of the amount of training they've undergone. That's because closing skills really can't be taught; they stem from innate personality traits. As a result, people either: (a) close prospects aggressively by repetitively asking for the sale and wearing the prospect down emotionally, or (b) make a logical case for why customers would want the product and then induce customers "close themselves."

Both styles work: There are too many fields of sales to isolate one closing style as *the* optimal manner for doing business. Although top producers usually fall into the former "aggressive closers" group, many successful salespeople are gentle persuaders as well (especially when dealing with more sophisticated clientele). The brand of closer that you want will ultimately depend on your product line and corporate culture.

Analyzing the Response

How to Get More Mileage Out of the Question. Candidates typically respond that they're capable of adapting their style of closing to a prospect's needs. Such a wishy-washy response does little to get to the heart of the matter: closing abilities. Of course, you will already have experienced the candidate's real-life closing skills firsthand in the previous role-plays about overcoming common objections and headhunting. Still, this self-appraisal query completes the picture by allowing the individual to explain why he considers himself a soft or a hard closer.

Therefore, to encourage a more detailed response, ask the candidate to grade his closing skills on a scale of 1 to 10 (10 being very aggressive, 1 being very benign). Such a weighted ranking exercise will result in responses like this:

> "I'd consider myself a 4, meaning that I don't really believe that aggressive closing tactics work in the field of employee benefits consulting. Clients expect their consultants to be excellent information and networking resources, so cold-call techniques and a transaction mentality simply won't work. Not that I can't make a strong recommendation to a client who's sitting on the fence regarding a certain issue. But you'll notice in my role-play of overcoming objections that I didn't push too hard on that first sales call. Building relationships takes time, and I'd rather nurture someone's business in small increments than aggressively push my way through the front door."

or

"I consider myself a 9 on a scale of 10. In auto sales, you've got to strike while the prospect is sitting in front of you. At our branch, statistics bore out that once customers walked out the door, they only had a 7 percent chance of returning. So if you didn't close them on the spot, you lost the sale. If my role-play appeared to be overly aggressive, it's because anything less would result in failure."

In addition, you might choose the following behavioral question to aid the candidate in this self-appraisal exercise: "How do you define hard versus soft selling? Give me an example of how you've handled both situations." In this instance, you'll solicit real-life stories from an applicant's past that reveal his inclination either to educate and gently persuade a customer (that is, a problem-solving, rational approach) or to push "reaction" buttons that appeal more to a prospect's emotions and fears.

Other questions to determine an individual's closing style include:

"Tell me about the last difficult sales negotiation you experienced. Could your sales manager have accused you of debating with customers rather than persuading them?"

"When is the last time you chose to stick to your guns and lose a sale? How do you determine when it's prudent to walk away from a deal?"

"Realistically assessing your style, do you find that you sometimes hesitate to ask for a sale? If so, what circumstances or kinds of people hold you back?"

46. All salespeople need to find an equilibrium between (a) high-volume production numbers and (b) quality. Which philosophy drives your sales style more?

Why Ask This Question?

Most salespeople will tell you that they're basically balanced in terms of harmonizing quality and quantity. Reality bears out a slightly different truth, however: Most people lean in one direction more than the other. Top producers are typically much more quantity-driven: They close deals and don't look backward. If they're lucky, they've got a great assistant to tie up the administrative loose ends. If not, they tie up their own loose ends when they get around to it . . . but not until all the deals that could possibly close that day or month are done!

Those who define themselves as more quality-driven, in comparison, usually close fewer deals, but all the details are neatly accounted for. They take the time to follow up with customers to ensure their satisfaction. Their paperwork trails are logical and easy to follow. And they pride themselves on building a solid referral base to ensure future business. Yes, it takes longer to make the sale for these individuals, but does the smaller volume potential mean any less of a return on investment for your company over the long haul?

Analyzing the Response

How to Get More Mileage Out of the Question. Only you can answer this question on the basis of your own sales style, corporate philosophy, and the amount of time you allow salespeople to show profitability. A smaller number of deals, however, doesn't necessarily equate with minimized revenues: If the profit-per-deal ratio is higher, then the number of deals closed becomes a secondary factor. Therefore, when employing this question, ask:

"Please distinguish the *quantity* of sales from the *profitability* per sale."

"Give me an example of your ability to structure high-point deals."

"What's the size of your average sale, and how could you have gotten more mileage out of it by selling more add-on products or configuring your mark-up differently?"

For example, in the mortgage lending business, subpar borrowers with poorer credit histories typically carry a greater risk that they won't repay their loans. To offset that additional risk, lending companies charge higher fees and percentage rates with variable payback terms. A loan officer who effectively structures higher point-deals—even though the volume of those transactions might be relatively low—ultimately rewards herself with higher commission earnings. A high-volume loan officer who structures fees below market, however, will typically earn very little above her base salary.

Therefore, to further confirm your insights, distinguish between the candidate's monthly guarantee and gross monthly earnings. The difference will be the commission payout, and it should typically at least double the base salary.

47. Tell me about the last time you failed to meet quota. How many times did that happen over the past year, and what plan of action did you take to get back on track?

Why Ask This Question?

The quality-quantity debate will always generate definitive insights into a candidate's way of doing business. When push comes to shove, however, sales boils down to hard-core numbers. You'll always read on a resumé about quotas exceeded and top production awards. However, you won't find out about the "hiccups" in the individual's production unless you ask.

Analyzing the Response

Failing to meet quota is nothing to be ashamed of if you're a salesperson. It's happened to everyone . . . a lot. "Racehorses"—performance-driven, short-term-minded people—work in sprints. "Plowhorses"—consistent billers—provide you with a consistent return, but rarely win the Kentucky Derby. The brand of salesperson you desire is up to you.

If the candidate had four or five inadequate months in a twelve-month period, you should be concerned. Meeting quota seventy percent of the time is probably a realistic expectation (although this can vary from industry to industry). Even if the candidate may bill well when he's hot, too many production gaps not only will lower aggregate annual production results, but they may also indicate problematic outside influences in the person's life, mood swings, and other inconsistencies that could negatively affect the team's performance.

How to Get More Mileage Out of the Question. If the candidate responds that there were no problems making quota, follow up by asking, "How much does your production vary from month to month?" Learn about production changes that might indicate large rises and falls (even though the falls never went below the quota threshold). Finally, if a candidate provides only a vague response, ask, "Doris, we're very thorough in terms of reference checking prospective new hires. How would your past supervisor at XYZ Company grade the fluctuations in your production? What would she say we could do to give you added support in that area?" Remember, asking candidates to volunteer shortcomings will provide you with a blueprint for future direction and focus.

48. With no undue flattery, if you will, grade me on how well I'm conducting this interview: What can you tell me about my sales and management style on the basis of the questions I'm asking you?

Why Ask This Question?

People-reading skills are critical to any sales executive's success. Because perception skills can't be taught by training, each candidate needs to have a fairly well defined ability to recognize strangers' personalities and business styles. Without that innate ability to adapt to another person's mode of communication, establishing rapport remains difficult, and sales opportunities will be missed. After all, the prospect shouldn't have to adopt herself to the salesperson's style: the salesperson is responsible for breaking through communication barriers and immediately establishing common ground.

Analyzing the Response

Testing an individual's people-reading skills should provide insights into how the candidate sizes up strangers. Since you're the only person that the two of you know in common, you might as well make yourself the focus of attention. This query will then reveal how accurately the candidate evaluates and bonds with newly introduced people on the spot.

How to Get More Mileage Out of the Question. Since the candidate needs to gauge your values as a manager to answer this question, save this query till the second half of the interview. Note the kinds of words the interviewee uses to describe you: "You're a really nice guy and you like your job" is a cop-out response because it's so superficial. Push the candidate further by asking for specifics regarding your management and sales styles:

"What would it be like working for me?"

"Where do you think I'd have the least amount of patience?"

"Tell me where I ranked as a salesperson when I was on the floor."

A candidate should be able to tell a lot about an interviewer by his attention to detail, his logical follow-up queries, and his questioning techniques. ("Behavior-based" interviewers, for example, come across a lot differently than "stress" interviewers.) Similarly, a sloppy office with mounds of paperwork makes a different impression from a neat office with neatly stacked files. These follow-up queries should consequently generate some firm responses from even the most gun-shy candidates. Their answers won't necessarily be correct, but there should be a logical basis for their responses.

Good Answers. For example, a perceptive response might sound like this:

"You're meticulous because everything is in order on your desk and on your bookshelf. You're taking lots of notes, so you obviously study applicants for later comparison and approach final decisions objectively once you've collected all the data. And just by asking this question, I see that you're not afraid of hearing rejections, so you obviously feel confident that you know your stuff. Finally, you listen very intently to every word that I say without finishing my sentences for me, so you've got excellent listening skills! I bet you expect the same kind of clean operation from your sales staff, so working with you would mean that I'd have to dot my i's and cross my t's."

Don't be surprised, by the way, to hear some undue flattery. Do, however, watch out for candidates who shower you with insincere, unfounded compliments. That's a sales style in and of itself, but that approach went the way of dinosaur once sophisticated consumers educated themselves and learned to avoid the "Slick Eddies" of this world.

49. How important is the base salary component to you? Would you prefer a straight commission if it offered you the potential for an additional 35 percent in aggregate earnings over the base salary?

Why Ask This Question?

Measuring candidates' risk factors says a lot about their sales mentality. Those who cling to high guarantees often come from conservative, risk-averse households where stability and steady income took precedence over risk-based earnings. These people have more of a "I work to live" attitude, and they typically see their work as a means to an end—namely, putting bread on the table.

In comparison, entrepreneurs "live to work" regardless of the amount of money they make. Their parents were most likely successful salespeople who opened their own businesses at fairly young ages and perhaps experienced a bankruptcy or two. The kids opened corner Kool-Aid stands once they turned five and have been "bitten by the profit bug" ever since. These are the people who never give up the helm of the ship even after they've made their millions. In short, they typically define themselves by the level of material success they generate.

Analyzing the Response

Distinguishing aggregate payout potential from guaranteed earnings could be telling. A salesperson with a husband, two children, and a mortgage may opt for a higher base pay with a lower payout potential because timing in her life dictates conservatism over risk. If that's the reason why this woman is sitting in your office for an interview (and you happen to offer the highest base pay program in town while all your competitors only offer straight commission), then you have lots to offer her. In this case, the problem that made her decide to leave her past company is solved by your organization.

RED FLAGS. If, on the other hand, you're interviewing someone who's fresh out of college, who considers himself a millionaire in the making, and who would opt for the $1,500 base plus minimal bonus over the straight commission package, then beware: You're probably looking at the classic risk-averse mentality mentioned previously. The moral of the story: Even if you don't offer a choice of earnings options (among base salary, commissions, and bonuses, for example), ask candidates how they'd ideally like to see their pay structured. Obviously, the higher the risk that candidates are willing to assume, the greater the reward for you and the aggregate payout for them.

50. Tell me about your quality ratios: How many prospects do you typically see before closing a sale?

Why Ask This Question?

Locking salespeople into a rhythm of activity dictates long-term success. Top producers focus on daily activity objectives rather than monthly production dollars because daily activities are in their control and production results are not. Once the salesperson identifies the necessary daily activity numbers that he needs to reach his production targets, you need to question his *quality ratios*. After all, the number of outbound phone calls and face-to-face sales presentations is limited. Tighter quality ratios, however, guarantee more results for the effort expended. Consequently, questioning an account executive regarding his activity level without balancing the equation from the perspective of quality ratios is the biggest mistake that sales interviewers make!

Analyzing the Response

Good Answers. The purpose of this exercise is to measure the candidate's understanding of her own quality ratios and the activity numbers she needs to make her monthly production quotas. The most practical way to apply this question is to ask the candidate to "reverse order" the activities necessary to make a sale. For example, a pharmaceuticals salesperson who is expected to sell $10,000 in prosthetic devices per month might answer the question this way:

> "The cost of an average prosthetic device that we sell is $2,000 to $3,000. To meet my monthly quota, therefore, I need to sell four products a month, or one a week. My ratio of presentations to sales is about fifty to one, so I need to visit about ten medical offices a day in order to make fifty presentations per week and, in turn, close one sale. So if my production ever drifts lower than it should, I make sure that I'm hitting my ten visits a day, and then I let my quality ratios take care of themselves."

RED FLAGS. Beware candidates who have difficulty articulating their quality ratios. Without a thorough understanding of the average activities necessary to generate a sale, there's a great chance that the candidate hasn't given enough thought to her trade. If that's the case, challenge the person to calculate on the spot the "numbers trail" that leads to closed deals. Take notes on her out-loud calculations to ensure that her estimates (and numeric reasoning skills) are accurate.

How to Get More Mileage Out of the Question. Finally, once those activity numbers are defined, query further: "If it takes fifty presentations to close one sale, what would you need to do to tighten your quality ratio to 45:1? How could I as your prospective sales manager strengthen your reward-to-effort ratio? How could you structure five more presentations per week to close more deals every year?" Combined with the candidate's production numbers, quality ratios will help you determine whether the individual focuses on high-payoff activities and maximizes her time.

51. How much does production vary from desk to desk in your office?

Why Ask This Question?

Identifying huge discrepancies in per-desk production averages may point to a serious issue known as the "rebel producer" syndrome. Rebel producers are very difficult to manage, and they destroy camaraderie and teamwork. Of course, determining how difficult an individual is to manage belongs in the reference-checking process. After all, previous managers will be much more forthcoming about a candidate's inclinations to undermine her peers than will the applicant herself. Still, allowing self-assessments in this critical area often points out problem situations that should be more fully explored in a background investigation.

Analyzing the Response

How do you know whether you've got a potential rebel producer on your hands? There are two telltale signs of this syndrome: (1) a distorted ratio of per-desk billings; and (2) a higher-than-expected turnover rate. For example, if you find out that the candidate in question produces 50 percent of her branch's revenues, your first reaction will be ecstatic: after all, you'll feel that you caught the goose that lays the golden egg! If a copier salesperson produces $600,000 of her branch's annual $1.2MM revenues, what could possibly be wrong with that?

After you think about it, though, you realize that this is a four-person office. If Kathy is generating $600,000 in revenues, then three other sales reps are only producing $600,000 among themselves: roughly $200,000 each. Since Kathy triples everyone else's production, ask her to account for the discrepancy. If all of her counterparts are trainees, then the disparity in billings certainly makes sense.

Kathy tells you, however, that everyone in the branch has similar tenure with the company. So why would the company keep all those underperformers who aren't making any money, you reason, when Kathy is holding the bar so high? Perhaps it's because she's a rebel producer who indeed makes a lot of money, but who, because of her insecurity, needs lots of "little failures" around her to convince her of her worth.

How to Get More Mileage Out of the Question. If you find such a gross disparity in production among staff members, you should deftly probe for more information: "Kathy, what are the typical problems and grievances that plague your branch, and what has employee turnover been like over the past two years?" You learn from this follow-up query that branch turnover is greater than 100 percent per year—far exceeding what you consider acceptable. When questioned about this enigma, Kathy has no response: Apparently everyone else out there is having problems keeping up with her and can't take the pressure.

CAUTION. These telltale signs point to a top producer with very little empathy for the people around her. They also point to a management team paralyzed by the rebel's production because she's keeping the branch alive. Is Kathy the wrong person for your organization? It's too early to tell. Instruct Kathy, however, that in checking references, you believe in talking not only with supervisors but with subordinates as well. Peers and subordinates in this case should be able to provide you with valuable insights into the individual's penchant for being a team player and maintaining a positive work environment.

Ending up with a high-need superstar could ruin all that you've built in a particular unit. It will cause conflict and turnover and, more significantly, impede your ability to attract other top producers. In short, your branch will never earn much more than that one producer's billings because you'll never be able to build a staff on that foundation.

Ten

Senior Management Evaluations: Leaders, Mentors, and Effective Decision Makers

Senior managerial candidates come in all shapes and sizes. Some want ultimate responsibility for their operations and insist on making all the decisions themselves. Others define themselves as fiercely loyal to their people and pride themselves on the teams they build by promoting their direct reports. Some march to their own drummers without necessarily linking their agendas to the company's bottom line. Still others are more comfortable not making waves and look for sign-off from above before implementing any new programs. These are all very human inclinations, but because senior managers maintain such a high profile in corporate America, their work habits and business philosophies warrant much closer scrutiny. Few people, after all, will be able to influence your corporate culture and increase top-line revenues more than your senior management team.

Only you know how to determine profitability for your particular line of business. This chapter will consequently focus not on the nuts and bolts of revenue generation but on the people issues surrounding candidates' actions. The challenge in any senior managerial interview is to create and maintain a balance between the macro business issues and the daily operational activities encountered by each candidate. That's because translating strategic issues into tactical objectives is the measuring rod against which managerial effectiveness is gauged. As a result, your interview questioning techniques should typically look for concrete examples of candidates' "people strategies" and their track records for influencing an organization's corporate culture.

52. Give me an example of your ability to facilitate progressive change within your organization.

Why Ask This Question?

Progressive change may certainly be evidenced by technological innovations in the workplace. That's especially the case when evaluating senior information technology candidates who focus their solutions on developing client servers, implementing predictive dialing units to increase outbound call volume exponentially, or automating manual systems in order to expand the organization's capacity for output.

Most senior managers outside of the data processing realm, however, will define their achievements by facilitating change according to productivity—not technological—issues. But before productivity changes can be determined, production measurements need to be established and then ratcheted up according to the talents of the workforce. Hence, real productivity change is often tied to new expectations established for the staff. Your focal point in assessing a candidate's response will consequently target *how* the individual achieved buy-in for the new programs and established more of a performance culture.

Analyzing the Response

Good Answers. How do senior executives implement change management? One of the ways is by making information available to everyone and creating an "intrepreneurial" mentality where workers assume ownership of their projects as if they were outside consultants bidding for the company's business. Another way is to give everyone a piece of the action and tie compensation to group performance as opposed to individual productivity. Similarly, look for executives who make organizational commitments to lifelong learning and a continuous improvement ethos by encouraging their staff members to further their own professional educations and in turn offer the company more creativity and innovation.

How to Get More Mileage Out of the Question. For example, let's assume you're interviewing a plant manager for your liquid and powder detergent manufacturing plant to streamline production procedures and increase plant productivity. The candidate has a track record for running a very productive operation at a competitor firm—a plant that was close to extinction before she came aboard. Your interviewing mission in this case, therefore, will be to learn how she diagnosed and solved production problems through people. You might ask:

"How did you gain a firm understanding of what was working and what wasn't when you first took over the plant?"

"How 'hands-on' were you in working the production line and sitting in on planning meetings with the engineers?"

"How were the ideas for streamlining production developed: Did you encourage team suggestions or have a mandate from headquarters to artificially impose new production standards?"

"What kind of resistance did you encounter from your existing staff?"

"What were the criteria you used in hiring new staff?"

"How did you improve the base line? Without thought to how the plant was currently processing soap products, what did you need to do to make the process better?"

"What kinds of cost factors did you consider in order to meet the organization's redefined needs?"

"How did you negotiate with corporate to attain the necessary improvements?"

"And finally, how effective were you at negotiating costs with vendors?"

This is an ideal setting, by the way, to implement behavioral questioning techniques:

"Tell me about your biggest obstacle—was it with people, budgets, or a stubborn and unyielding corporate culture? Give me an example of a reluctant compromise you had to make in order to reach your goal. How would the executive vice-president to whom you reported grade your accomplishments in that plant's transition? Give me an example of something you would do differently if you had the chance to do it all over again. . . ."

Does this seem like a lot to ask a candidate? Absolutely! But facilitating change is a lengthy process that defines itself by planned benchmarks and the attainment of preestablished goals. The people factor is critical at every step of the process, and this type of query allows you a window in which to measure the candidate's dealings with subordinates, superiors, and vendors. In short, it provides a prism through which you can see the future.

53. Tell me about the last time you inherited a problem unit—one suffering from poor productivity or low morale. What was the scope of the project, and how were your direct reports affected?

Why Ask This Question?

Every senior manager has a problem unit all the time: Even if things are going fairly well overall, then the unit with the least amount of output relative to its peers is de facto a problem unit. Dealing with a unit's problems might entail increasing employee morale, determining a unit's policies and procedures to provide clearer direction to staff and to avoid redundancies in job functions, reexamining the budgeting process to cost-justify ongoing programs, or revamping equipment and systems to bring a product more swiftly to market. Again, the focus in this issue will remain how managers accomplished their agendas through their people.

Analyzing the Response

Candidates typically have no problem painting a picture for you of a particular problem unit that they successfully turned around. Those "bragging rights" are often one of the first issues that candidates volunteer during an interview, and it's not uncommon to find them detailed on a resumé as well. Still, problem units more often than not stem from problem employees—ineffective middle managers who (1) don't believe in or don't understand the corporate mission statement, (2) doubt their ability to effectuate positive change in the organization, or (3) adhere more to an "entitlement" mentality and feel that they're owed a paycheck simply for showing up at work. These are all common scenarios that beg for effective management intervention.

Changing people's attitudes about work sometimes takes a carrot and sometimes takes a stick. Whatever the motivational means that senior managers use to change others' feelings about work, altering subordinates' behaviors and attitudes is one of the most challenging aspects facing management today. To complicate the problem even further, weak farm systems make it difficult for executives to weed out subpar performers aggressively.

How to Get More Mileage Out of the Question. A senior managerial candidate responsible for repairing a problem unit, however, will always need to remove middle managers with "incurable weaknesses." Therefore, this query often leads to situations where staff had to be cut. How those people were let go will tell you a lot about this individual's style of dealing with subordinates.

Some managers, for example, lop off heads. They're the "Bloody Marys" of corporate America who draw blood first and ask questions later. Others view the progressive discipline process as an opportunity to salvage subordinates via training (as opposed to a tool for getting rid of people). Whatever the case, question candidates about their opinions of how the terminations occurred:

> "How did your direct reports respond to your programs for changing production standards, motivating staff, and disposing of those who couldn't make the cut?"

> "How did you determine who should stay and who should go? What criteria did you use in the final analysis?"

> "What kinds of training programs did you install to aid your existing staff to meet your new performance initiatives?"

> "Tell me about your most difficult termination: What made it so hard, and how did you handle it?"

> "What kind of time frame benchmarks did you set for yourself, and how successful were you at reaching them?"

It's also logical for you to look for contrary evidence and ask for an example of a situation where the candidate wasn't successful at solving the problems that made a particular unit lag. No one can fix everything all the time, and it's interesting to hear about the times where the candidate was unable to manage the problem. Note what obstacles got in the individual's way, and examine them against your organization's current barriers.

54. Did you create a culture of open information sharing and increased accountability by giving responsibility to your subordinates, or did you focus more on establishing their parameters and controlling the decision-making process?

Why Ask This Question?

Senior managers affect your organization's corporate culture because they make an impact on the way people communicate with one another and feed information across departmental boundaries. On a broad behavioral spectrum, executives usually fall between two extremes: they either manage by consensus building and participative input from their subordinates, or they autocratically decide what is to be done and then force their mandates downward upon their staffs.

Of course, no one style is necessarily correct. And daily business life necessitates that a successful employee will be able to wield both styles of management depending upon the situation. Still, most people are inclined toward one way of supervising more than the other, and hiring the wrong style could create rifts in your senior management team. If, for example, you're used to running your company close to the vest and employing a "trickle down" theory of decision making, then the new hire who prides himself on empowering his direct reports and allowing them to operate autonomously may build resentment from other department heads. The centralized decision maker, conversely, in an open, "enlightened" environment may stir feelings of animosity in his direct reports, who feel as if they have chains around their necks.

Analyzing the Response

How to Get More Mileage Out of the Question. This query is fairly simple and practical to apply. As a self-appraisal query, ask the candidate:

> "On a scale of 1 to 10 (1 being that you have a totally autocratic style, 10 being that you make almost all your decisions by consulting with your staff and gaining their buy-in), how would you grade your decision-making style?"

Once the candidate admits that she's a 6 or a 4 (most people will take a middle-of-the-road response unless they know that you're specifically in the market for, say, a "Bloody Mary" type), question "What makes you a 4? If I were to check references with some of your direct reports, how would they grade you?"

Additionally you might ask:

> "If you're a 4 and naturally lean toward a more paternalistic, controlling style, what would make you a 1? In other words, what would drive you to the extreme of becoming a total autocrat? Give me an example of how that's played itself out in real life."

Reciprocally, you might question, "What could make you swing in the other direction and become a 6? When have you chosen to not follow your natural inclination in supervising others, and how did that work for you?" Finally, question, "What should I expect if we bring you aboard: You've been a 4 in the past; do you continue to see yourself that way, or is that natural inclination something you're seeking to change?" Forcing the numbers issue can be an effective way to assess candidates because it allows them to critically evaluate themselves and volunteer shortcomings.

55. How do you typically stay in the information loop and monitor your staff's performance?

Why Ask This Question?

Senior executives can't be everywhere all the time. Hence, many of them adopt a policy of hiring good managers beneath them and letting them manage. That's because the strength of the senior manager's directives is only as viable as the chain of command ordained to carry out those orders. Granted, insulation is a factor in any senior manager's life: there necessarily must be a distance between operative employees and key strategic decision makers. Time constraints ensure that. Still, no one should operate in total isolation. Therefore, mechanisms have to be put in place to feed information back to the source.

Analyzing the Response

Will a senior management candidate readily admit that she's too hands-off and doesn't have a total grasp on what's going on underneath her? Never . . . nor should she! Still, the way information gets fed back can be telling. The key to diagnosing the candidate's response is often found in the person's communications philosophy.

You've no doubt heard of "MBWA—Management by Walking Around." That can be a very viable style if the individual knows what she's looking for, has well developed intuitive skills, and has a knack for standing over people's shoulders and observing direct performance. Otherwise, it can merely be a façade with little value to the observer or the observees: after all, how much can anyone glean while casually walking through a department? Sure, this "slice of life" technique places the general among the infantry, but it's often the case that little more than a superficial observation is gained, and observers perceive the show of involvement as insincere.

What about managers who hold lots of meetings? Meetings can be very positive in that they allow staff members to share ideas, vent frustrations, and creatively brainstorm to customize solutions for the organization's changing needs. Meetings mandate communication, and there's typically not enough open information sharing in most organizations. On the other hand, meetings held too often can serve as superficial mechanisms that delay action and lead to analysis paralysis.

How to Get More Mileage Out of the Question. Therefore, question the perennial meeting holder like this:

> "John, what triggers your need for a staff meeting? Give me an example of the last meeting you held and who attended. What issues were tabled and what conclusions were reached? Tell me about a time when necessary action was postponed because you needed staff feedback before proceeding. How would your peers and superiors rate the value of your meetings?"

Managers who do have the inclination and time to work side by side with their troops make no bones about it. When senior vice-presidents of loan service sit down next to collections agents and crank out collections calls, those executives typically pride themselves on being in the trenches fighting alongside their troops. They feel that it builds loyalty among the ranks and keeps them close to the grassroots of their business. Is that the optimum management style? Again, that depends on your point of view and your particular line of business. Question the candidate:

> "How was your call to action perceived by your troops?"

> "Do you train people when you sit next to them and listen to them as well, or do you typically pick up the phone and do all the talking?"

> "What's the goal of this sit-in: Are you trying to instill a sense of camaraderie by working among the ranks, or is it more of a 'If I can do it, you can too' type of message you're sending?"

> "How do your peers regard your hands-on management style with your people?"

> "Give me an example of a time when a subordinate was embarrassed or otherwise uncomfortable with your actions when you were cranking out collections calls."

You can gain a lot of insight into candidates by gauging how they keep themselves in the daily communications flow and manage feedback. That's how corporate cultures are made and broken.

56. How do you typically confront subordinates when results are unacceptable?

Why Ask This Question?

Confronting problem employees is daunting for even the most confident managers. Some take a direct, unequivocal approach in delivering constructive criticism. Others provide a light and tactful touch and couch criticism in a context of warranted praise for work well done. Whatever your particular style, remember that many subordinates don't do what you *expect* but what you *inspect*. Therefore, imposing discipline on underperformers, setting well-defined objectives, and then policing the plan is a necessary part of everyday executive business life. The consequences of inaction, after all, could be perilous.

Analyzing the Response

The ability to distinguish sound supervisory approaches from ineffective ones reveals itself best through a behavioral questioning format. Bear in mind, however, that whatever response you get will call for a follow-up confirmation via a reference check. No one, after all, will describe his primary weakness as an avoidance of confrontation—that shows no backbone. On the other hand, candidates won't ever reveal their hot-headed tendencies lest they be perceived as undisciplined, reckless, and tactless. Outside third-party references will consequently offer more balanced insights into this touchy yet critical issue.

How to Get More Mileage Out of the Question. During your interview with the candidate, you might question:

"Tell me about a time when you had to be a strict disciplinarian."

"How swiftly will you resort to written documentation when a performance problem occurs?"

"Have you ever had to fire someone on the spot?"

"Would your boss ever describe you as a person who was more inclined to maintain smooth and amicable relations at the expense of avoiding confrontation at all costs?"

"Could a subordinate accuse you of being too heavy-handed and intent on pushing your agenda through with little regard for others' feelings?"

"Have you ever been accused of making unduly optimistic assumptions about your direct reports?"

"If you had to grade yourself on a scale of 1 to 5 (1 being you're a strict disciplinarian, 5 being you avoid confrontation at all costs), where would you fall on the spectrum? . . . What is it about you that makes you a 3? Tell me about the last time you had to show your teeth and turn into a 1."

There are obviously multiple ways to uncover a candidate's inclination to confront problem issues and stand up and fight. The key lies in allowing the individual to paint a picture of the circumstances and explain the necessity for taking such a strong course of action.

Eleven

Pressure Cooker Interview Questions: Assessing Grace Under Fire

One of the more common methods for measuring candidates' abilities to land on their feet is to challenge their assumptions and beliefs during the interview. Stress interviews per se intimidate candidates, squelch spontaneity, and consequently allow for little bonding and few shared insights. Asking a candidate, "Why shouldn't I hire you?" "Why aren't you making more money at this point in your career?" and "Why, with this resumé, would you see yourself as remotely qualified for this job?" only makes the person defensive and more inclined not to give you "real" answers. Besides, "if the interview seems like such a challenging obstacle, then imagine what the real job will be like!" goes the candidate's reasoning. In such circumstances, the carrot and stick routine will do little in the way of making the position or your company appear especially attractive.

So why this section in our book? First, because many employers still apply this methodology, it is important to evaluate and reexamine some of the more sophisticated pressure queries. Second, and more importantly, note that there is a big difference between *stress interviews* and *stress interview questions*. Every interviewer should be able to apply a pressure question when the need arises. That's especially the case when the position you're filling has lots of high-maintenance customers to tend to or if it historically suffers from high turnover. In such circumstances, a number of questions to test an individual's mettle might come in very handy. Furthermore, if you sense that a candidate is a little too cocky, then a skillfully placed pressure question could help humble him somewhat.

Following are some of the more effective "stress" queries that force individuals to volunteer self-critical insights. Remember again that an entire interview composed of such challenging queries will only cause ill will on the part of the candidate. So use them sparingly, but be prepared to pull one or two of these queries out of your hat when the situation arises.

57. Tell me about the your last performance appraisal. In which area were you most disappointed?

Why Ask This Question?

Remember that it is perfectly acceptable for you to request a candidate's most recent performance appraisal in the preemployment process. Many companies nowadays insert signature waivers in employment applications granting the company permission to check the candidate's past references. (Such releases are meant to remove, or at least minimize, the hiring company's exposure to claims of invasion of privacy or misuse of confidential information.) Similarly, a short paragraph in such a handout requesting a recent performance evaluation could go a long way in scaring off any mediocre performers. Handed out at the beginning of the interviewing process, that written notice will tie in well to this particular interviewing query because candidates realize that their interview responses will be substantiated when they turn their actual evaluations over to you at a later date.

Of course, no employee is perfect, so don't expect to find a halo around anyone's head. Still, some of the most graceful and polished interviewees may have committed some pretty egregious faux pas that will be reflected on paper. Knowing that they will have to present a recent performance evaluation as a condition of employment will go a long way in encouraging those candidates to speak openly about even the most uncomfortable performance situations.

Analyzing the Response

Performance appraisals historically addressed traits or work characteristics regarding an individual's cooperation, production, supervisory skills, and ability to get along with others. More progressive companies nowadays focus less on traits and features and more on specific perform-ance goals. For example, they may encourage employees to evaluate themselves in terms of areas where they have made the most impact on the company over the past year, areas where they need additional sup-port from management, and quarterly or annual goals that they wish to achieve with their managers' aid over the next evaluation period.

Whatever the appraisal methodology, it is important to evaluate can-didates' "measurement yardsticks" in their responses. When candidates come from companies that use traditional performance appraisals focus-ing on worker characteristics (like loyalty, dependability, and coopera-tion), then candidates' areas of disappointment will usually focus on disagreements they have with their *bosses'* perceptions. For example, you will hear the individual speak about his frustration at having only re-ceived a "good" instead of an "excellent" mark in one particular area.

When companies use more self-directed performance appraisal tech-niques (wherein they invite workers to identify their own performance goals and measurements), then candidates will often discuss their own *personal* disappointment at not meeting individually set objectives. The difference is worth noting because it will indicate the type of corporate culture the candidate comes from. Those from self-directed environments who were expected to set their own agendas and act autonomously are much more apt to assume responsibility for things gone wrong. They typically work with less supervision and structure because they are accus-tomed to higher individual and group performance expectations.

Good Answers. Whatever the orientation of the prior company's per-formance appraisal techniques, look for areas of performance weakness that are really "overstrengths," or virtues driven to an extreme. For exam-ple, someone censured for not delegating work appropriately or occasion-ally forging too far ahead of projects requires only mild tempering of his ambitions. In essence, those "weaknesses" hold a lot more future value than they do downside risk. In contrast, beware of the candidate who provides information regarding lackadaisical performance standards, low tolerance for adversity, or reliability problems. These problems typi-cally reveal themselves when candidates blame others for their own shortcomings.

Again, because candidates realize that they will have to provide an actual performance evaluation some time before you make them an offer, they will typically feel much more obliged to "come clean" regarding past indiscretions and failures.

58. In hindsight, how could you have improved your performance at your last position?

Why Ask This Question?

Even candidates with stellar performance evaluations would opt to rewrite history in light of their 20/20 hindsight. Improving performance is sometimes a factor of increased personal involvement. Sometimes it's a matter of wishing to change organizational limitations. Whatever the case, look for solutions in the candidate's response that show creativity and ingenuity in reframing problem issues and their outcomes.

Analyzing the Response

The ideal limitation in any employee's work history is time. High-performance job candidates do their jobs exceptionally well but continuously try to increase the impact of their results. Newly opened sales territories could be larger; reductions in departmental operating budgets could be deeper; new program launchings could have had greater market penetration. Accordingly, the hallmark of a high achiever's productivity is the desire to cut herself in half to capitalize on her accomplishments.

In addition, when a candidate provides you with a specific shortcoming in the previous query regarding performance appraisal disappointments, this natural follow-up demands (a) specific actions that reveal how the weaker performance could have been strengthened, and (b) the candidate's willingness to accept responsibility for things gone wrong. For example, you might ask, "Tell me, Dorothy, about your last performance appraisal. In which area were you most disappointed?" Dorothy, a human resources manager, responds that her greatest disappointment was in not reaching the goal she set for herself of lowering the company's cost per hire from $1,500 to $1,100. She instituted an internal referral program that she assumed would account for a 20 percent increase in staffing. Because of market conditions and less-than-ideal marketing of her plan to coworkers, the program never really took off.

How to Get More Mileage Out of the Question. Your follow-up sounds like this: "So tell me then, in hindsight, how could you have improved the results of that program?" Dorothy then explains:

"I still believe that the internal referral program could have been successful. I was told when I first proposed instituting the plan that it had been tried before and failed miserably. I wanted to prove them wrong because it had worked so well for me at my previous company. Still, my fate was somewhat sealed from the start in that my own boss predicted failure from the git-go. The marketing folks never seemed to get my ad copy into the monthly newsletter, and I consequently let the program drift. Still, I can't blame anyone else for the program's failure—it was my responsibility.

If I had to do it all again, I wouldn't have given credence to all those nay-sayers. I would have found ways to publicize the program myself via e-mail, the lunchroom bulletin board, and management training seminars. I learned that I shouldn't sit back and wait for others to do my bidding, especially when those folks aren't initially enthused about the prospects of the program. I got the okay to go ahead with it, and I accept responsibility for not having reached the program's goals."

Hence, the two key areas to look for in candidate responses focus on (1) what the candidate learned from the incident and (2) how willing the person was to accept responsibility for her actions. Both are earmarks of business maturity and reflect well on a candidate's objective self-evaluation skills.

59. Where do you disagree with your boss most often? How did you handle the last time she was wrong and you were right?

Why Ask This Question?

Differences in opinion are inevitable; conflict is optional. Still, there are times when conflict is forced upon you, and you have no option but to defend yourself. It's certainly difficult evaluating candidates' responses when it comes to addressing disagreements with their bosses. After all, you want someone who could stand up for himself. But you don't want someone who's too eager to draw lines in the sand and prepare for battle. As with all other moot responses that surface in a typical interview situation, if your gut tells you that you're getting less than the whole story, mark down your concerns in your notes so that you can address the issue from the other party's perspective via a reference check.

Candidates obviously feel challenged by such queries because respondents are forced to defend their actions unilaterally and pit themselves against the people to whom they should be most loyal: their bosses. Still, your question will surface extreme issues at the margin of that person's work history: namely, disagreement and disharmony with an immediate supervisor. Although you hope that such conflict is rare, it will inevitably face you one day if you hire this person, so it is useful to find out how she deals with it.

Analyzing the Response

Like many of our queries in this book, the two-pronged questioning pattern forces the interviewee to logically connect multiple facets of the issue at hand. Your first quest in gauging someone's response is to find out what kinds of issues trip the argument threshold. Next you want to see how the respondent relates to the supervisor when differences of opinion or outright discord occurs. The best way to bring this issue to the surface is to specify situations where the candidate was probably right and the superior wrong. That's because such situations will more clearly reveal the candidate's inclination to avoid confrontation, be humble about winning, or to "rub his boss's nose in it."

Disagreements usually occur for several reasons: Perhaps the candidate disagrees with his boss's opinions on how to best reach a predetermined business goal. Such dissension is usually technical in nature. More often an emotional disparity ignites the struggle. Such interpersonal conflict surfaces when a boss perceives her subordinate as overstepping his bounds; when a subordinate senses that a boss is not carrying her share of the workload; or when personal issues carry over into the work environment and staff members feel resentful of special exceptions made for certain people. Whatever the case, you should note whether there are technical or emotional lightning rods that bring about crisis in the candidate's work life.

RED FLAGS. Next, you need to examine how the candidate handles his boss's feelings after the conflict resolution. Responses like, "It turned out I was right after all. I had to be. It was obvious to me that she wasn't thinking the whole thing through" might leave you feeling a little ill at ease with the candidate's gloating. After all, even the best boss can't be right all the time. And you certainly don't want someone who's going to remind you of the times when you called the shots incorrectly.

Good Answers. If the true nature of the superior-subordinate relationship lies in complementing each others' strengths and supporting each others' weaknesses, then you'll want to find a subordinate who wants to keep the peace and who is able to maintain an objective perspective even in light of an all-out victory. In such cases, candidates' responses will sound much more conciliatory because they see the bigger picture of their actions:

> "Oh, I know that my boss would say that my decision, in retrospect, was more appropriate. But that's just because I dealt with that matter more often than she did, and I was better able to project the impact of that decision. But who's right and who's wrong is irrelevant; the point is, we made it through a difficult issue that was building pressure for quite a while. I think we both learned to respect each other's abilities a little more because of that conflict, and our relations since then have become a lot stronger."

Hiring a peacemaker makes a lot of sense when your goal is to maintain positive interpersonal relations with your staff. People who are at ease with themselves and keep an objective distance from the action will offer you a rational sounding board even when emotions are high. In the final analysis, it's not who's right or wrong: It's how the inevitable conflict gets resolved. The fewer the emotional battles and histrionics, the better. After all, you have a business to run!

Is this necessarily a "make it or break it" interview question? Probably not. Just be aware that you should be prepared to develop and cultivate a greater sense of objectivity in the candidate who's too focused on winning the battle. Because this person tends to focus more on *who* is right rather than *what* is right, he may have a tendency to divide rather than heal. Forewarned is forearmed, and the insight you gain from this question puts you in a better position for damage control.

60. How would your supervisor grade your ability to cope with last-minute change without breaking stride?

Why Ask This Question?

One of the greatest attributes of any employee at any level of the organization is the person's ability to be multitask-oriented. Certain people thrive in an environment of last-minute change, whereas others resent having the rug pulled out from underneath them as they attempt to accomplish a particular goal. If your environment necessitates quickly changing priorities and you hire the one-track, one-speed candidate, you might encounter resentment as the new hire interprets your shifting priorities as a poor, reactive management style. In such cases, you will probably end up spending more time counteracting the new hire's need for control, structure, and defined parameters than you would normally deem acceptable.

Analyzing the Response

This query could unnerve candidates who mentally operate on a more linear playing field and who dislike the lateral thinking involved in coordinating multiple tasks. It's difficult for candidates to proffer an encouraging answer when their inner conscience tells them that they need to avoid such situations. Therefore, you'll probably notice some discomfort in their responses and have your question immediately challenged:

"Oh, does this position require a lot of jumping around from task to task? Not that I mind; it's just that I prefer to complete one task before going on to another."

CAUTION. Careful now! If the candidate feels so strongly about this particular issue, it probably suggests that she worked before in an environment of quickly changing priorities where she was over her head. Your query simply sparked feelings of gross discomfort and sent up a signal flare in this individual's memory.

Your follow-up query will naturally attempt to probe for details using a behavioral questioning format:

"Tell me about the last time you felt as if you were over your head. Was it the changing priorities at work that made you uncomfortable, or was there some other reason?"

"How many balls in the air do you have at any given time, and how hectic a pace are you used to working at?"

"Do you prefer to tie together all the loose ends of project A and then move on to project B, or do you typically jump from project A to M, onto Z, and then back to A if time permits? Tell me how a situation like that actually played itself out in the past."

In these cases, the behavioral interviewing format demands that the candidate weaves a tale of dealing with pressure and setting priorities when few structural systems are in place. As with all series of behavioral questions, inconsistencies may surface in the responses if candidates weave a tall tale with little basis in fact. Further, if you sense a low tolerance for dealing with changing priorities in the person's response, then add this query to your reference-checking activities to gain objective, third-party insights into the matter.

Interviews should be challenging meetings focused on discovering the real person behind the resumé. A little discomfort is not necessarily a bad thing. The strategy is to balance your investigation so that candidates feel welcome to share insights with you freely while you gather authentic data about their strengths, weaknesses, inclinations, and dislikes.

Twelve

Generic Interview Questions Known to Challenge Candidates in the Final Rounds of Hire

Sometimes the most enlightening queries are the simplest. The purpose of this book is to look at various types of questioning techniques to meet the specific demands of particular hiring situations. And although these specific interviewing insights help you define and refine your choices from the broad spectrum of available candidates, it remains critical to balance your approach with some good old-fashioned "horse sense" queries.

The following questions are the ones that register more in a candidate's stomach than in his head. That's because they're so broad that they're usually difficult for candidates to put their hands around. Hence, they make candidates feel a little awkward. After all, when an individual is totally geared up for a big interview, has studied your annual report, and has prepared detailed responses regarding his career management successes and failures, it could get a little cumbersome to answer something as seemingly mundane as "Why do you want to work here?"

The purpose of the question is not to unnerve the candidate. It is, instead, meant to evaluate the individual's gut responses to seemingly obvious issues. Consequently, no interview preparation book is complete without a look at these generic questioning challenges. These are, after all, the old hard-core interviewing questions that have been used for years by staunch businesspeople who want immediate bottom-line responses. One caveat, though: These questions work best in the final rounds of hire. Only after job candidates have met with a number of potential coworkers and heard several versions of the organization's challenges and focus will they be in a position to address the following broad-based queries.

61. Why do you want to work here?

Why Ask This Question?

Have you ever heard someone say something along the lines of, "Well, I really need a job so that I don't lose my house, and you're the closest I've gotten to being hired in the last thirty-seven interviews"? Perhaps you might admire the person's honesty, but you know that such a candid response isn't going to catapult this individual's career to new heights! As a matter of fact, anyone who hints that he just can't seem to find work throws up a red flag in even the most empathetic interviewer's mind. After all, if no other employers out there seem to find this person worthy of hire, maybe they're all seeing something that you're not, right?

And desperation to pay bills is never a valid reason for a candidate to accept a job because once the immediacy of the acute financial pain subsides, that candidate will be off again wanting to get back on the fast track. . . . most likely outside of your company! So what should you be listening for in a solid response?

Analyzing the Response

Good Answers. By the time the candidate's gotten through four rounds of meetings with your staff, she'd better have some clear insights into why she wants to come to work for you and what she can contribute. Candidates will typically link their desire to join a particular company to one of three things:

1. *The company:* its reputation as a quality employer, its high-profile brand-name recognition, or the fact that the organization is growing rapidly and perhaps offers a ground-floor opportunity to help the company grow.
2. *The position:* its variety, pace, reporting relationships, technical orientation, or scope of authority.
3. *The people:* a personality match reveals itself via a feeling of acceptance and the fact that the candidate believes she'll fit in and her contributions will be recognized.

Individuals who compliment any of these things show respect and admiration for the organization and ultimately reveal a valid desire to join your team. They will have provided an excellent response to an awfully generic query that might have tripped them up had they not given some prior thoughts to why they want to work for you.

RED FLAGS. On the other hand, you may hear some responses that scare you off from an otherwise successful interview. Candidates should typically articulate what they could do for the company, not what the company could do for them. (Forgive the twist on John F. Kennedy's words!) Consequently, individuals who strictly limit their answers to what *they* want to get out of the relationship weaken their cases. For example, people who say they want to come to work for you because your benefits are outstanding, you pay higher than your competitors, or because you're known for aggressively promoting from within create a selfish perception about themselves and offer your organization very little initial goodwill.

After all, benefits packages change. Similarly, if a candidate is solely motivated by money, he may end up as recruiter's bait, staying only until a higher-paying position surfaces elsewhere. And if a candidate appears overly interested in being promoted to a higher position before even being hired for the job at hand, then he may have premature assumptions about moving up the ladder after only six months of employment—long before you'll have had the chance to gain some stability and continuity in that position you filled.

There's nothing more irritating than having a recent new hire constantly reminding you that he needs more challenge from a higher position within the company. You'll reason that he shouldn't have accepted your position in the first place if his real intention was to seek higher levels of responsibility. In short, his real reason for leaving his present company will most likely recur at your organization over the long haul.

CAUTION. Note as well that this issue typically surfaces when a prospective new hire prepares to take a significant salary cut by joining your firm. ("Significant," in this case, means a greater than 20 percent reduction in salary.) Let's say that an office manager lost her $45,000-a-year job with a Big 6 CPA firm eight months ago and has had a difficult time finding work because everyone tells her she's overqualified and that organizations aren't creating a lot of middle-management, administrative supervisory roles. Well, she doesn't feel that she's overqualified at all. And she certainly doesn't think that anyone else should be attempting to crawl inside her brain in order to make decisions about her based on what *they* think she's thinking!

Still, offering this candidate a $30,000-a-year executive secretarial position should throw up some red flags for you. First, although she is probably being very honest and open with herself and you about wanting to get back to work even if it means accepting a position with less money, glamour, and responsibility, human nature predicts that she'll eventually want to get back to her previous salary range and status. But salary and status are only symptoms of the real malady: You could end up hiring someone who has matured (in a business sense) beyond those lesser responsibilities. That's the real problem!

Let's say, for instance, that this candidate was promoted into office management five years ago, leaving behind the tasks associated with hands-on secretarial assignments. If that's the case, she may have stretched her "mental rubber band" to a salary range, status, and level of responsibility and challenge that your secretarial position simply cannot fulfill. Your job will in essence only provide her with a back-up to put bread on the table. Hence, her accepting your position may be nothing more than a "been there, done that" proposition to tide her over for a while. There's definitely not a lot of potential for a long-term successful relationship here.

You may argue that such an otherwise successful worker deserves another chance at building her career again. After all, just because corporate America lost a lot of its midsection in the "Nasty Nineties" doesn't mean that people like this office manager should be disenfranchised. Indeed, she may be more motivated than most to roll up her sleeves and find new ways of contributing to her next company. These are all very valid issues, and you have to let your conscience be your guide when hiring people whose positions were eliminated through no fault of their own. But such hires deserve extra special consideration lest you become victim of a candidate wanting to park her wagon in your lot for the meantime while exploring options with greater career potential outside your company.

62. What do you know about our company?

Why Ask This Question?

Oh, that's an easy one! I've heard candidates respond with answers anywhere on the spectrum from "You're a bank" to "I researched your organization very thoroughly, and I read that you were founded in 1913 under a thrift charter, went public in 1919 at a share price of $8, and then went on to benefit from the post–World War I lending climate by. . . ."

Okay, I'm being facetious—it's not really an easy query. If the candidate's too generic and unable to paint a picture of the organization's place in its market, its uniqueness, its corporate mission and culture, then that individual may lack the critical global reasoning and research skills necessary to provide solutions to your problems. On the other hand, if the interviewee goes into too much detail about issues that have very little bearing on the organization's challenges today, then you might reason that he's a pedant who lays undue emphasis on less-than-critical issues. Either way, the candidate loses.

Analyzing the Response

Good Answers. What should you expect in a well-balanced response? A well-informed candidate should be able to rattle off the demographics fairly quickly and then get to the meat of the issue: what your organization does differently from its competitors and what challenges you face in your changing market. As a quick checklist to the first issue, any finalist candidate at the middle-management level or in the sales arena should be able to identify the following issues about your organization:

- Year founded
- Headquarters location
- Number of employees
- Revenues, assets under management, size of government grant
- Primary and secondary product markets and lines
- Computer systems
- Exchanges where the company's stock is traded

Even administrative support staff and clerical candidates should have developed an overall understanding of your company's particular line of business by the final round of interview. It's not unrealistic on your part to expect a stock or mailroom clerk to be able to articulate such issues, especially if your first-line interviewers provide handouts about the firm. Note that the depth of their understanding of these broader issues is not what is at question here: Instead, it is their interest in the job and their desire to impress you that matters most.

The second issue is a little bit more challenging: *line* managers who are directly responsible for increasing your organization's top-line revenues must clearly understand and be able to articulate where your industry is in its development, where your organization fits within that industry, and what new areas of market penetration need to be exploited and developed in order to maintain profitability. Line managers, therefore, must be challenged to articulate what solutions they can provide on the basis of their experiences working for your competitors. Because they are "insiders," they should be much more forthcoming in terms of mapping out specific directions and plans to guide your company's growth.

In contrast, *staff* managers like those found in accounting, information technology, and human resources—the noncore segments of a business—will typically have less of an understanding of your company's or industry's current state of affairs. In return, however, they will bring with them a particular specialty that supports your organization's core business activities. Expect staffers to focus more on the demographic information mentioned earlier: material that can be researched in the library should suffice to convince you that the candidate values your time so much that she was willing to learn about your organization (as an "outsider") in every way possible.

63. Tell me about your understanding of the job you're applying for.

Why Ask This Question?

Similarly to the preceding question, trying to answer this query in thirty seconds or less can be harrowing for any candidate. Attempting to regurgitate everything the person has learned through library research and four previous rounds of interviews can make even the most organized applicant gulp. What counts, after all, is the individual's ability to synthesize mounds of information on the spot and prioritize key issues quickly. Since this kind of question is often used to open up a final round of interviews, there will be a little more pressure on the individual to make the right impression on you. So don't hold it against finalists who sweat while articulating their responses: They just want to make a favorable impression!

Analyzing the Response

Good Answers. What should you expect in a well-balanced response this time? A well-informed candidate should be able to rattle off the following issues clearly:

- The position's title
- Its reporting relationship upward on both a straight- and dotted-line (indirect) basis
- Its reporting relationship downward (that is, the numbers and titles of direct and extended reports)
- The position's primary duties
- Its secondary responsibilities
- The reason the position is open
- Its key challenges within the first ninety days or one year
- The problem the company is trying to solve by hiring someone new

Obviously, the information flows from the very specific and concrete (the position's title and reporting relationships) to the broader implications of providing a solution to the organization's needs. Here's how it sounds in real life from a candidate for an information technology (IT) position:

"Dennis, I understand that this is a newly created position for a computer operations manager to report directly to you, the IT director. Apparently, you've decided to create this new job to prepare for a systems conversion from your HP3000 platform to a UNIX client server environment. Therefore, you're looking for someone skilled in that target software area.

I also came to learn that you feel that creating a new operations managership will relieve the workloads of three people— you, the VP of information technologies, and the current operations manager, whose background lies more along the programming lines than along traditional operations lines.

Anyway, you've got a staff of forty people who almost all come from HP3000 backgrounds. Your biggest challenge in addition to preparing for the conversion to UNIX lies in simply keeping up with the workload as your organization opens its first operations in Canada and Mexico. And the person you hire will have to be a high-output production person who's sensitive to the current strain on the organization due to both the company's growth spurt and the introduction of a new software system.

I'd like to think, Dennis, that I'm prepared to meet those challenges and offer solutions to your key needs. . . ."

Bravo! A very well-rounded yet specific rendition of identifying the organization's wound, so to speak, and then preparing to provide a particular solution to heal the wound.

64. What can you do for us if we hire you, and when should we expect to see concrete results?

Why Ask This Question?

The first three questions in this chapter probe for an individual's ability to comprehend the overall picture and then point out areas of focus and concern for you, the hiring manager. This query presents a very practical follow-up technique to bring closure to those previous queries. For example, now that you know why the individual wants to join your team and what he has learned about your company and the position via research and previous rounds of interviews, you need to see how he will specifically solve your problems. In gauging this answer, you'll also gain critical insights into why accepting this position would make sense for him from a career management standpoint.

Analyzing the Response

The first rule in assessing this critical response is to look beyond the "perfect match syndrome." Many hiring managers mistakenly look for a 100 percent match between a candidate's experiences and skills and their companies' immediate needs. Yes, it would be great to bring aboard someone who could come aboard immediately as an up-and-running problem solver. But that role should be reserved for outside consultants. Instead, you should be looking for a 70 to 80 percent fit so that the individual has room to grow within your firm. Only then will you be offering the candidate a chance to develop greater skills and build a stronger inventory of achievements—which is the glue that binds people to any company.

CAUTION. The second rule in evaluating candidates' responses focuses on the amount of concrete information provided. Look for candidates who are willing to show you their cards in terms of how they'll attempt to address particular issues. People who shy away from sharing with you their approaches for improving your work environment reveal little goodwill in the preemployment process. Yes, the candidate runs the risk of having one of his ideas stolen—especially if you don't hire him. And yes, there is a chance that what he sees as a potential solution might not be exactly what you had in mind. But those risks are more than offset by his refusing to accept your invitation to brainstorm and problem-solve.

In the case of the computer operations manager discussed above, it is critical that this individual accept your invitation to spell out potential solutions for your firm's needs. After all, he did an excellent job gathering the data necessary to complete the picture of why this newly created position has developed. He pointed out the department's discomfort with the UNIX software conversion process since most of the staff members were HP3000 specialists. He readily identified the stress and strain felt by everyone as the company grew rapidly on the information technology group's back. And he pinpointed the fact that this new position could relieve the workloads of three coworkers. These are all excellent insights, but it's obviously the third issue that begs for more clarification. So here's how the candidate continued:

> "Dennis, the VP of the information technology group is clearly more concerned with the strategic issues of determining the organization's changing needs as you move into the international arena. You, as director, have worked on a UNIX client server platform, but as the only key player in the organization to do that, you'll need someone to relieve you of that sole burden. And your current operations manager comes out of the programming and analysis environment more than a traditional operations school, so we would complement each other well.
>
> My first area of focus would be on clearing a path for data conversion. I've got a solid UNIX client server background, and I'd suggest possibly holding weekly meetings with the staff for the first quarter to keep a tight handle on problems that surface.
>
> Next, I'm more than willing to lend an extra hand in any areas where the workload is overwhelming. I have no problems sitting down and coding all day, and even though that's something I've long since outgrown from a career standpoint, it sounds as if now you need someone to fill in the gaps.
>
> Finally, I believe that within ninety days we'll have laid the groundwork to begin the data conversion process, and the entire program could be managed within six to eight months. Again, I want to be a part of an organization with national expansion plans, and overseeing a software conversion of this size would be the ultimate challenge to me. . . ."

Obviously, you may not have the same plans for this candidate. As a matter of fact, your priorities may lie in a totally different direction. But his willingness to share his expertise and point out priorities that *he* feels you'd want most is the ultimate in goodwill and open information sharing. The key issue is not necessarily that you both agree on what gets done and when—that can be decided once the new hire comes aboard. The critical nature of this response, however, has to do with the fact that this person will risk being wrong to help you make an open and honest assessment of him. Such candid offerings typically have very positive results over the long term. Hence, putting a candidate in the position to share some of his expertise and project target completion dates may reveal a lot about the individual's style, communication skills, and organizational forecasting ability.

PART II

Selecting Candidates and Making the Offer

Thirteen

Reference-Checking Scenarios: Administrative Support Staff

Administrative support reference questions focus primarily on superior-subordinate relationships in terms of how candidates follow instructions, work independently, respond to constructive criticism, and feed information back to you. The career opportunities for secretaries, administrative assistants, and other members of the administrative support ranks offer more variety, reward, and independent decision making than ever. Consequently, the talent emerging from their ranks is nothing less than astounding. As a result, you'll need to sharpen your referencing skills to separate excellence from mediocrity. These questions for candidates' former supervisors will be an excellent place to start.

65. How structured an environment would you say this individual needs to reach her maximum potential?

Why Ask This Question?

This supervisory issue is always surfaced first in the reference-checking process because it gets former employers talking freely. Since it requires an objective response with no right or wrong answers, an employer won't initially feel as if he's playing God with the former employee's future by having to immediately address weaknesses and shortcomings. (Those issues will follow shortly.) More importantly, this query provides future advice on how to bring out the best in the individual. You'll have a lot more success getting people to speak about future guidance issues rather than past performance problems because it places past employers in a mentoring role capable of adding valuable career advice.

Analyzing the Response

Some people require fairly structured direction with lots of feedback and ongoing open communication. Others work much more efficiently when their bosses simply set the parameters for a project and leave them alone to complete their work independently. Again, this is a matter of style, so there is no right or wrong answer. Many managers feel that option 2—total independence—is the ideal response. That's because most people want some kind of assurance that they won't have to baby-sit a demanding new employee.

Although that's generally true, the best answer simply hinges upon your personal management style. If you like working fairly independently without a lot of interaction with your staff, then such a response would be great. On the other hand, if you have trouble totally letting go of projects under your control, you'll probably want your subordinates to keep you in the progress loop as if you were still in control. Hence, you'd probably prefer working with a subordinate who enjoys ongoing direction and feedback because it keeps you tuned in to what's happening.

Remember that the purpose of the reference check is not solely to determine a candidate's "hirability" vis-à-vis past performance issues. The best references, in contrast, provide insights and future direction for giving the new hire added support from day one. This way, no one has to reinvent the wheel in terms of meshing personal styles with business cultures.

How to Get More Mileage Out of the Question. There is a variation on this theme that you might favor as a first question in the reference-checking process:

> "John, you're Doug's past boss, and if all goes well, I'll be his next supervisor. My management style is to be fairly 'laissez-faire' in the sense that I really cherish my time and independence. Some people might consider that a weakness of mine, but I don't want to provide a lot of structure and direction to my staff. I guess I value their independence as much as I cherish my own, and I expect them to complete their projects all by themselves. How would Doug fare under my type of management style?"

This scenario is a little bit more like *Jeopardy* in that you're providing the answer and looking for someone to tell you the question. The results you get, though, should be equally valuable. If you use no other reference-check question in the preemployment hiring process, use this one because it will provide you with some very important information about the optimal management style for a prospective new hire.

66. Does this individual typically adhere strictly to job duties, or does he assume responsibilities beyond the basic, written job description?

Why Ask This Question?

As a second question out of the starting gate, this one should again prompt the past supervisor to talk openly about the candidate's work ethic. The "entitlement" mentality of "I'm owed a job" and "I don't do windows" is totally out of sync with today's high-demand jobs. Indeed, for the first time in American business history, large companies forced to downsize are looking more at performance than at tenure in deciding who makes the final cut. And in a radical and aggressive business environment that defines itself as streamlined, lean and mean, responsive to change, and globally competitive, increasing productivity per employee has become the key mechanism for companies to maintain a competitive edge.

Analyzing the Response

Good Answers. This is a very appropriate query for gauging administrative support candidates because it paints an immediate picture of an individual's values. One of the best pieces of feedback you'll generate will sound like this:

> "The clock never stops for this guy. He's always looking for more things to do when things slow down in his area. More importantly, he has a sense of urgency and immediacy that gets things happening. It's the pace and commitment to results that make him a natural at customer service both with internal and external clients. . . ."

Other times, you will find that *everyone* at a particular company is so overloaded that assuming additional responsibilities is really a nonissue.

Because of understaffing, people are working through their lunches, committing themselves to unlimited overtime on last-minute notice, and are barely keeping pace with the existing workload. Still, when a past employer provides that kind of description of the business environment, it's fairly safe to assume that the candidate will have little problem keeping up with you if your organization moves at a fast clip.

RED FLAGS. On the other hand, you will sometimes receive responses that politely brush around the issue:

> "Well, I can't say I really expected him to do anything above and beyond the call of duty. He does his job, and he does it well. But I wouldn't expect him to go looking for more just because it gets slow in the office all of a sudden. I don't expect my people to 'go out of the box' and get creative on me in terms of doing others' work for them, so my answer to your question is no. . . ."

Would you hire this person or keep looking for someone else? The answer, again, is simple—it depends. Although this book focuses on identifying high-performance individuals who are top producers in their respective disciplines, not every job requires a hero. Some positions simply need "worker bees," the types of folks who never seem to tire of highly repetitive tasks. And if that's your mandate for the next opening you need to fill, then don't be turned off by a response that provides little enthusiasm for a track record of assuming greater responsibilities. Workers who do their jobs and go home, after all, have a place in many companies. Just be sure you're matching the right type of individual to that kind of job.

67. Please comment on this person's ability to accept constructive criticism.

Why Ask This Question?

This is another showstopper that will gather data pertinent to your future management of this individual. First, identify your own style of providing constructive criticism right now. And be honest—it might not be "constructive" at all. If you have difficulty communicating with people because you have a short fuse when things go wrong, then emphasize in your interviews and reference checks that you don't have lots of patience and need someone who's fairly thick-skinned and who doesn't take things personally. In contrast, if you've been in situations before where you felt that your subordinates took advantage of your good nature, then ask about the candidate's inclination to shortcut the system when the boss isn't around.

Analyzing the Response

How to Get More Mileage Out of the Question. It is not uncommon to weigh this issue against all else in the selection process. Oversensitivity in a subordinate, after all, is the last thing that many managers want. For example, you might approach the whole issue of discipline during your interview this way:

> "Jim, if you're not thick-skinned and can't take it right between the eyes, then I'm not the right boss for you. I don't have a lot of time to coddle my staff, and I won't worry about hurting your feelings if anything hits the fan. This is business, and I want results, not excuses."

Similarly, you could explain your supervisory approach to a former employer during a reference check and ask:

> "I'll be candid with you regarding one of my key concerns in adding a new member to my support staff. I'm fairly short-tempered, and I don't always say thank you. I don't want to have to mince words or worry about others' feelings being hurt. I've left out the issue of oversensitivity when hiring in the past and found out the hard way that I had to walk on eggshells around the new hire for the duration of that person's tenure. Can I get right to the point with Jim when there's a problem, or would he have problems working for someone as demanding and direct as I am?"

At the administrative support level, hurt feelings and a sense of being put down and underappreciated are some of the most common reasons why employees leave companies in pursuit of greener pastures. By all means, don't leave this issue in the "wait and see" column of your hiring checklist. Identify the candidate's capacity for taking it on the chin before you say "I do" to a new employment arrangement.

On the other hand, if you recognize too much tolerance in your own management style and fear being taken advantage of, ask:

"I'm not an overly aggressive manager, and I've been somewhat taken advantage of in the past. I don't particularly like confronting problem employees, so I try to hire very independent types who don't rely on my being present to get work done. How independently will Jim work? How inclined is he to take advantage of another person or situation when the opportunity arises?"

When your concerns are openly shared this way, you'll generate very straightforward responses that provide optimal insights into managing this person.

68. How much do outside influences play a role in her job performance?

Why Ask This Question?

This query lends itself best to administrative support workers who are often younger, less experienced, and less balanced in their lives and careers than their more senior counterparts. Just because immaturity is a part of growing up doesn't mean that you have to bear the burden of the individual's coming of age! Work is a significant rite of passage in a person's life, but that empathetic notion aside, you don't want to be caught in the middle when someone is in the process of deciding what role work should play relative to her personal life.

You've no doubt heard of an otherwise successful hire being derailed by boyfriend or girlfriend problems. Or maybe everything's going great, but 9:00 A.M. seems to come earlier every morning for a new hire preoccupied with too many nocturnal alliances. If your company's hiring strategy is to employ very early career people who have minimal experience and salary requirements, then grab onto this query and employ it religiously!

Analyzing the Response

CAUTION. How honest will past employers be regarding a subordinate's extracurricular activities? It depends on the past supervisor and the nature of the problems vis-à-vis their impact on job performance. And that's very important to keep in mind. Just as in an interview, you don't want to know about personal problems outside the office that have no bearing on the individual's job performance. That's an invasion of privacy and may well end up compromising mechanisms for employee protection contained in the Americans with Disabilities Act, the Family Medical Leave Act, and other employee rights safeguards. Make no bones about sharing with a reference contact that you want only job-related information. If unrelated information is unintentionally volunteered, keep it in perspective and, by all means, don't write it down!

One final point here: Historical problems are not necessarily clear indicators of an individual's future work performance. People change by learning from their mistakes. So the individual with the tardy problem because of late-night soirees might have graduated from school or relocated away from old friends. The man who couldn't seem to locate a stable apartment and consistently needed to leave work early to apartment-hunt might indeed have established some roots. And the lady who was preoccupied with incoming calls all day from her mother who was having serious troubles with the IRS may have resolved those issues by now.

In all fairness to yourself and the candidate, therefore, delve more deeply into the resolution of any problems. Ask past employers whether they're aware of the problem being resolved. In some cases, you might even want to call the candidate yourself and ask him to address the status of those issues. In that case, you'll be establishing a relationship based on open communications and simultaneously setting your future performance expectations in one fell swoop.

69. Would you consider this individual more of a task-oriented or project-oriented worker?

Why Ask This Question?

Task orientation lends itself more to the clerical-level job opening, where work instructions are dictated from above and followed rigidly. Project orientation involves much more freedom, independent decision making, and discretion to reach targeted goals. The work mode that you desire simply depends on the amount of autonomy you want the individual to exercise in the overall decision-making process.

Analyzing the Response

Past bosses typically respond to this question very subjectively. If the past worker exercised a fair amount of discretion on the job and was capable of moving from point A to point C while delegating someone else to tie up the loose ends at point B, he will be categorized as a project-oriented individual. Note, however, that even if the person holds the title of executive secretary or administrative assistant (titles you would expect to be more project-oriented), he may be categorized as a task-oriented worker by his previous employer. Why? Because titles don't necessarily depict assertiveness, independence, or project-management orientation. Don't forget that this is a highly subjective definition.

Some administrative support employees come from environments that strongly discourage independent decision making. Thus, they are conditioned to obtain waves of sign-offs from their superiors before venturing into even common activities. When this is the case—even though the employee is acting according to company mandates—this individual will still be described as task-oriented. This doesn't mean that he couldn't handle project work independently; it's simply that the person wasn't given the opportunity to exercise much discretion.

Why is this significant? If you feel you've interviewed someone whose title should correspond with more of a project orientation, and the supervisor classifies this candidate as task-oriented, it's probably worth your while to question the employer about her company's expectations and how *she* defines task versus project orientation. The extra clarification could explain the former supervisor's subjective interpretation.

70. How does he handle interruptions, breaks in routine, and last-minute changes?

Why Ask This Question?

This is the foundation of the administrative support worker in corporate America: flexibility, adaptability, and multitask orientation. Any kind of superior-subordinate relationship requires the subordination of one party's needs to the other's—especially in an intimate working relationship with a personal or administrative assistant. Of course, staff accountants need to subordinate their needs to the demands of the accounting manager. But such relationships are typically less dependent upon each other and allow for greater flexibility in response time. So use this question when evaluating workers whose schedules and priorities will need to mirror yours rather closely.

Analyzing the Response

There are two basic ways that people coordinate the activities on their desks. Some need to complete one project and tie up all the loose ends before moving on to another task. Others pride themselves on their ability to juggle multiple tasks and keep a number of balls in the air simultaneously. Obviously, those who fit the second profile typically respond to last-minute changes more effectively than those who innately need to complete one task before moving on to another.

How to Get More Mileage Out of the Question. You might also ask the former supervisor a question along the lines of:

> "Maggie, my needs change on a dime, and I really would be a challenging boss if I hired someone who got flustered under pressure. How does a break in the routine throw George off? What's the worst scenario you could think of where he really became unwound by a last-minute change?"

This question adds a behavioral element to your reference check in that you ask for concrete, historical evidence of how the candidate performed on the job. Behavioral formats work very well in reference checks just as they do in interviews, so apply this technique for your really important issues.

71. How would you grade her commitment to project completion?

Why Ask This Question?

Administrative support workers may be task-oriented or they may be project-oriented. They may assume a strict interpretation of their job responsibilities or demonstrate a mentality for "going outside of the box." They may require a structured environment with lots of feedback and direction or a very hands-off management style to succeed. But the bottom line is that projects must be completed on time and accurately. There is simply no excuse for mediocre work product.

Analyzing the Response

Project completion means follow-through. You've probably supervised people who walked around the office with legal pads jotting down anything and everything that needed to be done as ideas came to them. You've most likely also supervised people who had the best intentions of seeing a project through to completion but who tried to keep everything in their heads no matter how quickly you threw new information their way.

Most managers are big fans of daily planners and "To Do" lists because they represent physical proof that new information is being stored for future action. Of course, people have different capacities for staying on top of their work. However, you'll most likely have more empathy for the employee who writes something down and doesn't get to it than for the worker who simply forgets details of particular assignments. If detailed follow-through is a critical skill that will separate winners from losers in your business, then run this question up the flagpole to see what results you gather.

How to Get More Mileage Out of the Question. If a past employer says that the individual's follow-through could be better, question:

- "Give me an example of the types of assignments she falls down on. Are they immediate tasks that don't get done, or does Mary Jo have difficulty completing longer-term projects?"
- "Does Mary Jo write her planned activities down on a 'To Do' list, and if not, would that kind of time management tool help?"
- "How 'fixable' is the problem? Is it a matter of her not understanding what's expected of her? Does she have problems comprehending the work in general? Or does she simply forget?"
- "How committed is she to developing better follow-through skills?"

By using these kinds of qualifying questions, you should be better prepared to dissect responses that beg for more clarity.

Fourteen

Reference-Checking Scenarios: Professional/ Technical Candidates

The reference-checking questions that follow will allow you to continue in your quest to gain third-party, objective information regarding an individual's ability to excel in your company. Bear in mind, though, that critical queries for professional and technical candidates go beyond what is listed below. These queries are useful and practical in terms of gauging candidates' historical work patterns and providing future insights regarding optimal management techniques. However, they necessarily lack the specific details unique to your industry or discipline. Only you can develop adequate questions to measure a candidate's specific performance in a number of given areas.

For example, if you are checking references on a residential real estate appraiser, you'll probably want to address these position-specific issues:

"What were the daily production standards at your firm in terms of full-blown, Fannie Mae appraisals versus limited, drive-by appraisals?"

"How would you grade the candidate's narrative skills?"

"How consistent was she at selecting adequate comps for a given property?"

"How willing was he to handle appraisals in dilapidated structures or generally go beyond the call of duty?"

Similarly, if you're staffing openings for insurance claims adjusters, you might ask:

"What was the size of the typical caseload assigned to the individual?"

"How aggressive was this adjustor at auditing medical bills and setting adequate reserves for a given claim?"

"Would you consider the candidate a soft negotiator who backed down from a confrontation with an aggressive attorney, or did she show a stubborn resistance toward settling beyond a predetermined limit?"

The specific nature of these questions depends on your particular business and industry. The key to developing such queries lies in assessing the skills that your most successful staff members have in common as well as the knockout factors that have historically made people fail at the job. The development of such a skills- or performance-based inventory is a simple and straightforward exercise, and such questions will definitely complement the queries that follow.

72. How would you grade this candidate's capacity for analytical thinking and problem solving?

Why Ask This Question?

It's probably uncomfortable for you to just come out and ask how smart somebody is. You also don't want to lob a query like, "Does Jane have a good head on her shoulders?" because people are predisposed to say yes to such general issues. After all, a former employer who says no to that kind of question would not only be guaranteeing that Jane loses out on your company's job offer, but he would also insult his own management skills for having hired Jane in the first place.

Still, you have a right to know whether someone is predisposed to react with emotions instead of reason. You might learn that the individual has a restless nature and is easily sidetracked, distracted, or bored. Perhaps the candidate in question is opinionated and argumentative, and such an inclination impedes her ability to solve problems analytically and objectively. Additionally, you may hear that the individual is overly optimistic about how quickly and easily things can be made to happen; therefore, she spreads herself too thin and makes unduly optimistic assumptions about her subordinates' abilities without developing contingency plans.

Analyzing the Response

In essence, this query demands a response to: "How well does this person know her business?" You're not necessarily gauging IQS or natural propensities for genius. In contrast, this is a hands-on question regarding the candidate's ability to distinguish sound decisions from ineffective ones. And expertise in decision making is more a function of exposure and experience than of natural intelligence. After all, no senior manager will have risen through the ranks of middle management without having had his nose bloodied somewhat. And we all learn more from our mistakes than from our successes anyway.

RED FLAGS. Still, analytical thinking demands business maturity, solid listening skills, and a propensity to project the consequences of one's actions. It stems from self-confidence and awareness of personal limitations. Therefore, when interpreting the feedback you get, look out for problematic responses that point to an irrational, shoot-from-the-hip mentality. The problematic feedback you get might sound like this:

> "Oh, Dave is a very good underwriter, but he sometimes over-commits himself because he wears rose-colored glasses and is overly optimistic as to what can be accomplished in a given day."

or

> "Rachel makes a fine corporate attorney, but it's only been two years since she graduated from law school, and I think she's still contemplating where she can make the biggest impact in the legal field in general. Her calling may be outside the corporate world, such as working for a nonprofit organization, and the fact that she grapples with a 'higher cause' in all her actions can blur her ability to make effective and sound decisions."

or

> "I've addressed this issue with Sharon before, and I feel that although she's very smart, her lack of organization puts her in a position to put out fires all the time rather than work proactively at staying ahead of problems before they surface. She doesn't always structure her plans for working through a project. That's impeded her ability to solve problems as effectively as she other-

wise could, so that's an area where you'd definitely want to give her added support and structure."

Such feedback will merit closer scrutiny as you speak with other references.

73. Does this individual need close supervision to excel, or does she take more of an autonomous, independent approach to her work?

Why Ask This Question?

Some people naturally like to work in groups or "pods," side by side with their peers. They crave recognition for a job well done, and they enjoy ongoing social interaction. For them work is all about deriving a psychic income from developing other people's skills and abilities as they move through corporate America fulfilling their own life's agenda. These people will keep their managers in the loop regarding the status on a given project because they feel that their managers have a right to know. This way, those managers don't have to worry about the individual's performance, and there's ample reason for social interaction.

On the other side of the spectrum, you'll find the loners—the folks with a fierce level of independence who cherish the freedom to get work done their way above all else. If you oversupervise such employees, you will be accused of being a micromanager and being distrustful of them. Why else, goes their reasoning, would you need to be on top of them so much? "If you trusted me and my work, you would allow me to come to you when I had a problem." Interaction above that level is simply uncalled for.

Analyzing the Response

Not to overgeneralize categories of workers out there, but you'll often be able to distinguish between affiliative and analytical types of people. Affiliative types always focus on the people factor in business situations. Their primary concerns revolve around their coworker relationships: personal disappointments and surprises, feelings regarding people's perceptions about their work, and an interest in others' career and personal development. These are the folks who immediately identify themselves as "people persons" and who place fellow workers' needs above profits or other business concerns.

Analytical types, in comparison, value their own freedom and the ability to work independently. They often see little need to get too close to coworkers. Accountants, architects, and computer programmers who sit in front of PCS all day creating solutions to complex problems are usually analytical kinds of people. These types of independent thinkers are usually the ones with the greatest need for autonomy and freedom.

The feedback you'll get regarding analytical types during a reference check will sound like this:

> "He works best in an environment where you're not looking over his shoulder. He's not a yes-man by any stretch of the imagination. He'll creatively get things done, he'll reinvent the wheel if need be, and he'll constantly network and develop new alliances. But he's got to have the latitude to reach his goals. If you oversupervise him, you'll squelch the enthusiasm and creativity that makes him happy and keeps him producing."

It is ultimately your choice to hire either kind of person. Be especially aware, however, of hiring analytical types if you prefer to provide lots of structure, direction, and feedback on a day-to-day basis. Your natural style of management and goodwill may be perceived as burdensome to the solo flyer. In that case, recognize your own need to control situations and your preference for keeping your people on a short leash, and hire accordingly.

74. How global a perspective does he have? Do you see him eventually making the transition from a tactical and operational career path to the strategic level necessary for a career in senior management?

Why Ask This Question?

The ability to see beyond immediate areas of impact and scope of responsibility helps middle managers move up through the ranks within their own departments. It also prepares department heads to climb successfully to higher realms of corporate accountability. Consequently, it becomes important in evaluating professional and technical candidates to measure how much the Peter Principle has played a role in their careers. The concept behind this principle is that those who are "Petered out" have simply risen in the organization to a level where they are incompetent, and this precludes their climbing any further.

Analyzing the Response

There's nothing wrong with reaching such a plateau in anyone's career. After all, most people aren't cut out to be CEOs of Fortune 500 companies. As a matter of fact, you may view the Peter Principle as a practical necessity of business life that ensures continuity in the positions you're filling. After all, if you need a controller to head up a section of your accounting department, you might not really want a candidate who sees herself becoming your organization's next CFO. Not that becoming a CFO isn't a noble aspiration: It's just that it can become uncomfortable trying to placate someone who wants too much too fast. And there are few managers out there who haven't had to face that leapfrog syndrome before.

Of course, others hope to reach their first chief financial officership via a steady and planned progression through the ranks. They realize that it could take ten years in a company to reach that goal and are willing to build a list of credentials that ultimately qualifies them for such responsibility. More importantly, they are realistic about the time and energy commitment necessary to achieve their plan. You certainly can't take away from someone the fact that the person is realistically building a foundation for greater responsibilities.

How to Get More Mileage Out of the Question. But what about those candidates who see themselves achieving grand career achievements but who lack the requisite talent or commitment to make that happen? That's what you want to find out via this reference-checking question! Follow up your initial query with a qualifying statement like:

> "Eileen, could someone argue that Diane is 'Petered out' as a controller in the sense that she's really reached her maximum ability to make an impact on your company, or do you see her as an up-and-comer with a lot more potential to take on more global responsibilities?"

If Eileen responds that Diane is an up-and-comer, you could in turn qualify that response with the follow-up:

> "That's great, but I don't want to hire someone who's itching to move through the ranks prematurely. Is she prepared to spend three more years as a controller, or do you sense that she's more

aggressive in wanting to reach certain goals in a shorter time frame?"

That generic add-on query should suffice to provide you with an insight into the individual's career expectations and ability to stick it out with your company over the long haul.

75. How would you grade this candidate's listening skills?

Why Ask This Question?

The difference between hearing and listening is that hearing simply entails sound waves bouncing off a person's eardrum and then resonating through the cranial bones a little bit. Listening, on the other hand, is a much more mentally engaging activity, demanding that an individual make an effort to internalize those sound waves and interpret the message sent to his brain in order to make some kind of decision. Listening is therefore an active process that requires energy and willingness on the part of the receiver.

Still, there are some humans out there who listen but refuse to hear what you're saying. That's because they typically choose to do things their own way and selectively hear what is most convenient. I assume you can think of at least one such specimen in your life! The question is, How do you identify these selective listeners via a reference check?

Analyzing the Response

RED FLAGS. When asking this question, beware the respondent who goes overboard at impressing upon you the need to be clear in your dealings with the candidate. For example, you might get a response like this:

> "Paul, David has to have a blueprint of your needs or else he'll go off and make all the decisions himself. What worked best for me was repeating, 'This is what we agreed to,' 'Let's go back over this to make sure it's clear,' and 'I want to make sure that there's no ambiguity here: Tell me again your understanding of what I want.' "

Wow! Are you getting the message? This past employer is painting a picture of throttling this guy who's obviously burned that past employer on occasion by not following instructions. To be fair in my treatment of this particular case, the employer continued his response by stating:

"Without such specific directions on your part, he'll make all the calls himself the way he sees fit. Not that he's a poor decision maker—on the contrary, he's very capable and competent. Still, you just can't expect him to follow your directions for arriving at the finish line unless you're absolutely clear from the beginning."

Obviously, that qualifier redeemed the candidate somewhat. But this response points out that there may be mental tugs-of-war with a selective listener bent on manipulating the rules to his own liking. Is this a matter of poor listening skills or a determined desire to carry out one's own agenda? You'll never know. Just remember that you're not questioning whether the person needs a hearing aid. Instead, you're delicately probing to find out how insistent and strong-willed the person is by nature to circumvent your authority.

76. How effective is the candidate at delivering bad news? Will he typically assume responsibility for things gone wrong?

Why Ask This Question?

Thank goodness most people fall into the middle of the spectrum when it comes to assuming responsibility for mistakes. At the far end of the spectrum lie the martyrs: the people who take blame for everything even when they have little control or direct responsibility over the outcome. At the other extreme are the Teflon managers who are never at fault for anything: It's their supervisors, leads, technicians, and secretaries who blow it all the time.

Hmmm. Which one bothers you more? You'd probably prefer the martyr to the Teflon manager. That's because the majority of businesspeople would agree that nothing is more reprehensible than failure to assume appropriate responsibility for things gone wrong. Locating this tragic flaw in the reference-checking process is indeed difficult. But since it's pretty much impossible to locate such information during an interview and because personality tests typically can't judge this particular issue, the reference-checking process is the only medium available in which to generate candid feedback.

Analyzing the Response

How to Get More Mileage Out of the Question. You might choose to let the question stand on its own. The silence following your question, after all, can be a powerful tool that demands an honest response. On the other hand, you could employ a situational questioning style that throws the past employer into a quasi-real business scenario like this:

> "Michelle, Charlotte is your lead HVAC engineer. If the machines on the assembly line run a little too hot and the filled liquid containers coming out the other side end up with uneven distributions, does Charlotte turn into a martyr who accepts total responsibility for the whole team, or is she inclined to become a Teflon engineer who has a tendency to find fault with others?"

A tepid and apologetic response saying, "Well, I don't want to say that she lays all the blame on everyone else, but she does have some difficulty accepting total responsibility for her team's output" is the red flag that begs for further explanation. Press further:

> "What would her subordinates say about that? Is it a matter of an overinflated ego, or would you say that it's a fear of loss that dictates her response? Has she ever had occasion to 'throw a subordinate under the bus' to free herself of responsibility?"

Again, remember that this is a very difficult issue for employers to address. It's an ugly characteristic of what may otherwise be a very successful management candidate. Still, if your previous employee had a tendency to undercut his staff's loyalty by hedging his involvement in his unit's shortcomings, then you'll want to cover this issue in checking the backgrounds of all finalist candidates.

Note that if one supervisor tips you off that this serious problem may exist, then you'll want to speak with other past superiors regarding the issue. In addition, it would make sense to conduct subordinate references, which seek to gauge the candidate's management style from the bottom up. Subordinates will typically be a lot more forthcoming in sharing information regarding a manager who places blame disproportionately on the more helpless members of the staff.

77. Please grade the individual's capacity for initiative and taking action. Does she have a tendency to get bogged down in "analysis paralysis"?

Why Ask This Question?

It is not uncommon for specialists in analytical disciplines to demonstrate substantial resistance to predicting final outcomes. After all, business is a practiced art of weighing risks and rewards by maximizing growth opportunities and hedging downside uncertainties. And with so much information available from computer databases and the Internet, making the final call can become rather difficult as mounds of evidence pile up for or against certain options. Place this "information overload" formula into a business environment that demands a consistent track record for making the right choices, and you'll end up with pressured and stressed-out executives who are gun-shy of making final determinations.

Still, right or wrong isn't always the primary issue: The consequences of inaction could lead to an even more significant erosion of confidence in your organization's credibility and viability. So like it or not, "analysis paralysis" isn't an option even if you're the most caring and empathetic employer in the world.

Analyzing the Response

This scenario is the opposite of when candidates "shoot from the hip." Just as you want to avoid those folks who play loose and hard with the facts and "shoot first, ask questions later," you need to elude those who never shoot the gun at all. The problem with the hip-shooters is that they don't thoroughly measure the consequences of their actions before making a decision. The problem with the procrastinators is that they dissect the possible outcomes of their decisions to a point where they get frozen like deer in an oncoming car's headlights. Not always, of course . . . but in enough situations (or in one critical instance) to make the former supervisor label the individual as gun-shy when the heat's on.

How to Get More Mileage Out of the Question. An excellent way to play this issue out in the reference-checking process is to force a comparison (rather than ask for a cut-and-dried, one-way-or-the-other outcome). Here's an alternative way to ask the question or follow up when the employer is having difficulty interpreting what you want to find out:

> "Larry, every employer in the world wants to find that perfect balance of decision makers: folks who don't shoot from the hip without measuring the consequences of their actions, and people who don't lack self-confidence when it comes time to make the tough calls. Still, most people lean toward one extreme more

than the other. Would you say that Heidi is more of a hip shooter or perhaps someone who gets bogged down in the details and has difficulty making a final decision?"

If you receive a benign response stating that Heidi never shoots without aiming and equally has no problem making the tough calls, then conclude that this issue will not adversely affect the candidate's performance. If, on the other hand, the past employer raises serious issues regarding the candidate's tendency to leap without looking or to freeze up from the pressures of taking definitive action after analyzing complex information, then reexamine the individual's candidacy. If your style will temper the individual's approach toward decision making, then your being forewarned will put you in a better position to provide added support immediately. If not, then realize that your decision-making styles are incompatible and move on to your next candidate.

Fifteen

Reference-Checking Scenarios: Senior Management Candidates

How difficult is it to gather critical background data on senior management candidates in the reference-checking process? Well, it's not as difficult as you'd think, considering that most higher-level executives are wise enough to realize that providing reference feedback for a peer is nothing short of career insurance. After all, a quirky twist of fate may have that past supervisor depending on his subordinate for career opportunities in the future.

Combine this with the fact that senior managers don't get the same drill from human resources departments regarding the legal pitfalls and judicial exposure associated with providing reference feedback (HR's dictates, after all, won't always carry all the way to the executive suite), and you'll see why many senior managers are willing to share their opinions freely and help out peers and subordinates who are in career transition. It's simply in everyone's best interests to say good things about a fellow executive who—"there but for the grace of God go I"—has the misfortune of being terminated because of political upheaval, management change, or lackluster stock performance.

However, even though senior managers are willing to talk, they can sometimes "sugarcoat" their responses. Again, what goes around comes around in the inner sanctum of the executive suite, and competitors today may be allies tomorrow. Consequently, you may end up with an overly optimistic picture of a candidate's performance because of this unspoken "gentleman's agreement" to aid others in transition. Therefore, it becomes critical that you fine-tune your questions in the reference-checking process to highlight performance and style issues that otherwise might be covered up with a polite and safe, "Oh, Ralph is great, and he'll do a wonderful job for you" response.

78. Is this candidate's management style more autocratic and paternalistic or is it geared toward a more participative and consensus-building approach?

Why Ask This Question?

We know that individuals influence corporate cultures. We also know that senior managers, more so than anyone else in the organization, set the formal tone within their divisions for internal communications, problem solving, performance expectations, sign-off procedures, and accountability. Employ this query first in the reference-checking process to get straight to the people skills issue. The response you generate will set the tone for all the answers to follow. (After all, if you find out that the candidate takes a "my way or the highway" approach to problem solving, that will most likely color the rest of the responses you get.) This is also a question that typically gets employers talking freely because it commands a very subjective and fairly "safe" response.

Analyzing the Response

How to Get More Mileage Out of the Question. Let's assume you get an answer that sounds fairly noncommittal:

> "Peggy can be an autocrat when she needs to achieve a definitive goal in a short amount of time, but she also encourages her subordinates to chip in when the situation calls for it."

Well, the fact that this past superior points out Peggy's flexibility is a good sign that her management style isn't too autocratic or too laissez-faire.

To encourage more specific feedback, however, focus the employer on the number of meetings the candidate holds on a regular basis. In general, senior managers who hold few if any meetings with their direct or extended reports tend to govern a little bit more unilaterally than most. After all, if participative input isn't called for, there will be little opportunity to benefit from others' suggestions.

In contrast, senior managers who strive to orchestrate the combined activities of direct reports by holding lots of meetings, cross-training their teams, or job-swapping lower-level staff members so that workers more clearly understand their internal clients' needs obviously depend more on consensus building and buy-in at the grassroots level. Again, there's no right or wrong answer here. It's simply a matter of encouraging the respondent to be more descriptive in her interpretation of your question.

79. In terms of this individual's energy level, how would you grade his capacity for hustle?

Why Ask This Question?

Capacity for hustle relates to the abundant reserves of energy that an individual has to draw upon. Increased speed in daily activities doesn't necessarily equate to higher-quality output or more effective decision making. Indeed, the most effective decision makers may be the most reluctant to commit to a final resolution. Still, this query may raise two issues that are critical to you in the selection process: First, you are looking for compatibility issues when bringing someone new aboard: compatible decision-making styles, communication approaches, mentoring philosophies, and speed in processing information. Second, you might find out via this reference-checking query that an individual suffers somewhat from "analysis paralysis," meaning that he has a tendency to get bogged down in minute details rather than look at the big picture.

Is either issue a deal breaker? Of course not. If you happen to move very quickly and you find out that this vice-president who will report to you is much slower to come to a decision, you might appreciate the fact that he will most likely temper your inclination to move too rapidly or to make overly optimistic assumptions about the market or your staff's ability to reach a predetermined goal. Similarly, if you could be accused of bordering on the more cautious side, then a sidekick who is quicker to the draw might add an extra level of "umph" to your own management style.

The bottom line remains the same: These background investigations you're carrying out serve as objective evidence that should convince you that a particular candidate's needs will not exceed available "corporate resources" (like your time and patience!).

Analyzing the Response

How to Get More Mileage Out of the Question. We profiled earlier (see Question 41 in Chapter 8) how to question candidates' preferences for their desired pace. We also helped interviewees respond to your question by delineating three speeds from which to choose: (a) a moderate, controllable, and predictable environment; (b) a faster-paced atmosphere driven by occasional deadline pressures; or (c) a hyperspace, crisis" mode, as you'd expect to find on the floor of a stock exchange. These very same choices may be shared with the individual who's providing you with reference feedback about a senior management candidate. After all, they certainly help to paint a vivid picture of what "hustle" means to you, and that clarity of definition might come in handy in assisting the other party to interpret your question.

Remember as well that capacity for hustle speaks to going above and beyond the call of duty on last-minute notice. Such actions represent nothing less than an individual's pride in work and commitment to a job well done. Consequently, a response along the lines of "She's not going to move too fast for you—that's just the way she is" might call into question the candidate's enthusiasm for her chosen career path or her resilience in coping with adversity. In such a case, the response you receive could very well reveal that an applicant is unmotivated, tired, bored, or otherwise burned out.

80. How does this individual approach taking action without getting prior approval?

Why Ask This Question?

RED FLAGS. Who was it that said, "Never ask for permission . . . just ask for forgiveness"? Well, whoever it was, it's a good thing he never worked for your company, right? Actually, taking unilateral action is called for practically on a daily basis. No senior manager could have risen through the ranks without the ability to call the shots independently on occasion, and without a track record for calling the *right* shots the majority of the time. Still, there are rebels. These folks pride themselves on doing things their own way. They are "intrepreneurs" in every sense of the word—they may work for you and be on your payroll, but they run that company as if it were their own. And that fierce defiance sometimes looks for opportunities to express itself.

Whether you want that brand of self-reliance and autonomy depends on what you need to achieve by bringing the new hire aboard. This one particular aspect, however, could have terrible ramifications if a new hire is marching out of step with the rest of your management team. Feelings of anger, jealousy, and favoritism will inevitably develop among peers, and lines of demarcation will be drawn that force your team to form camps of allies. Your culture will have been violated, and you will be immediately forced either to censure this new rebel or to give him a lot of backing and support—much to the chagrin of your existing staff, who have been playing by the rules the whole time. Such issues guarantee one swift result: lower employee morale.

Analyzing the Response

How to Get More Mileage Out of the Question. As with many of our interviewing and reference-checking questions, it is often best to employ behavioral interviewing techniques in gauging responses. In this instance, you should explain your concerns first and then invite the past superior to comment on the candidate's ability to meet your needs. For example, you might say to Nina Rose, Acme Corporation's chief financial officer:

> "Nina, I need a vice-president of finance who obviously has the ability to make effective decisions independently, but I can't have a rebel who looks for opportunities to take action without getting my prior approval. I've suffered from that rebel syndrome before, and it just goes against my style of running a business. Would you give me an example of a time when Sam Paul could've gotten prior approval from you and didn't? Was it inappropriate, and should he have known better?"

By clearly articulating your needs and asking for a concrete historical issue to demonstrate the candidate's inclination to "shoot from the hip" and bypass the proper channels of communication, you'll not only gauge whether the candidate would inappropriately jump the gun, but how flagrant the incident really was. Again, because of the critical impact this one issue could have on your organization's performance, it is worth the time employing a behavioral questioning format to more clearly understand the ramifications of the candidate's past actions.

81. Is it this person's natural inclination to report to someone else for sign-off, or does she operate better with independent responsibility and authority?

Why Ask This Question?

This is a natural follow-up query to the previous question if you want even more objective feedback to measure the individual's inclination to follow all the rules or occasionally strike out on his own by making new rules.

Analyzing the Response

How to Get More Mileage Out of the Question. Here's how it works. Let's say you've asked the first query in this two-question string like this: "Nina, how does Sam approach the issue of taking action without getting prior approval?" Nina responds, "He's an effective decision maker, and he won't go out of his way to step out of line. He's got a healthy ego, but it's not so big that he needs to prove his authority by circumventing your procedures."

Your natural follow-up would be:

"Great, Nina, I'm glad to hear that. Let me ask you this: In terms of giving him the proper managerial support from day one, should I expect him to come to me for sign-off because he feels protected by doing that, or is Sam better off if I simply give him as much responsibility and authority as possible right up front?"

And voilà—you should generate a very honest and open answer regarding Sam's feelings toward being supervised. After all, your questions show nothing but concern for getting this new hire off on the right foot. Hence, you'll gain reliable third-party data with which you can also make a more effective hiring decision.

82. After so many years in the business, is this candidate still on a career track for which she can sustain enthusiasm?

Why Ask This Question?

Our introduction into this query—"after so many years in the business"—is a function of senior management in general. You simply don't get to the top unless you've spent years learning your business inside and out. The latter part of the question—"is the candidate still on a career track for which she can sustain enthusiasm"—is a euphemism for "Is this candidate burned out on the business?" It's a practical question that's worded nicely.

The point is that there are lots of mentally unemployed folks out there. They're still generating paychecks for themselves. They might even be looking for greener pastures by coming to you on an exploratory basis. However, they may be looking because their ticket is about to be punched at their current company, and they simply can't afford to be laid off for too long. There's nothing else they can do to earn the kind of money they're earning, but their hearts just aren't in it anymore.

Analyzing the Response

Interestingly enough, while other questions in the reference-checking process may run smoothly along, this one particular query often throws respondents into a quasi-confession mode. That's because it usually hits the nail on the head by making the former supervisor admit that the real problem lies in the individual's staying power. There's just not a lot of fight left in this person because plastics manufacturing has just gotten too predictable. The challenge is gone, the fun has long since passed. The person finds himself at a career juncture where he either has to get off the train and adjust to a much more modest lifestyle (because of severely reduced earnings) or he's got to smile, "suck it up," and get back aboard for another trip around the tracks.

How to Get More Mileage Out of the Question. When you sense the hesitation in the past supervisor's voice, ask:

> "I know that Chuck's sole focus in his career up to now has been in general management at plastics plants. Would he rather be doing something else? I mean besides lying on the beach in Hawaii, does he live for his outside interests? Has he fallen out of love with the business?"

Of course, such prodding could lead to some very candid insights that go beyond strictly work-related issues. Still, work never exists in a vacuum—it's only one element of the total person. Note as well that this issue has little to do with a candidate's age. Spending eighteen years in plastics manufacturing could be a very long time for a thirty-six-year-old.

Gathering this information is critical because you inject a very serious element of risk into the picture when the candidate needs to work but doesn't really want to. Not to get too philosophical here, but you very well may be doing that individual a favor by not hiring him so that he could put that terminable career issue to rest and then be free to "begin the first day of the rest of his life." No one, after all, lives to work and foregoes all other outside interests.

But when candidates have an overwhelming need to find satisfaction totally beyond the work place, they may have difficulties making a break with their careers because of guilt or social pressures. Still, similar to early career job-hoppers, they have to kiss some frogs before they find their prince. You don't have to be one of those frogs! In this case, although the candidate may have mentally made the break with his career (that's now earning him $125,000 a year), he's not going to tell you that. An objective third-party reference, however, may be more forthcoming.

83. How effective is this person at orchestrating a corporate ensemble of functional areas?

Why Ask This Question?

Higher-level managers often oversee multiple functional areas. The lines of supervision may be direct or indirect, but the bottom line is that the organizational chart can only point to one ultimate source of responsibility. Line (revenue-producing) and staff (noncore, operational, and supportive) functions work together just like woodwinds, brass, and strings in a symphony. But what can separate a sleepy little company from a lean performer poised for growth is often a management team's shared understanding and appreciation of what it takes to run the company from a more global perspective. Senior managers must consequently see to it that their direct reports understand the financial end of the business and comprehend the way their departments connect to the rest of the company.

Analyzing the Response

This query is probably the most lofty of all the questions put forth in this book. After all, if the person weren't successful at coordinating an ensemble of functional areas—in other words, managing—then she should be in a different line of business! The application of this question, however, isn't so grand and lofty as you might think. Its real focus is to identify a senior management candidate's inclination toward open financials and economic advocacy—that is, the individual's willingness to share profit and loss information and company performance status with the rest of the management team.

It is not uncommon in small, privately held companies for owners to guard the books rigidly. "Employees don't need to know how the company is doing—they just need to do their jobs" is the hard-line mantra taken toward information sharing. Publicly traded companies, on the other hand, legally have to make financial performance data available. That includes documenting the number of shares of common stock the CEO has outstanding as well as the makeup of key executives' compensation packages. Still, even if the information is public, that doesn't mean that an organization will purposely disclose such data to employees. After all, if employees don't know to look at 10K, 10Q, and proxy statement filings, then they're none the worse for wear, right?

Although it's not uncommon for companies to maintain a veil of secrecy around corporate performance, cutting-edge organizations with enlightened management teams voluntarily involve their managers in global performance issues. The logic goes that if all the employees see which way the ship is sailing, then they'll have a greater understanding of how their masts should be strung. And should the ship suddenly change course, they will be able to adapt more quickly to the captain's new needs if they're aware of the overall goal.

How to Get More Mileage Out of the Question. Therefore, to make this seemingly lofty query a practical tool in the reference-checking process, ask a past superior:

"As CFO, Dave Tolle was overseeing human resources, the information technology group, accounting, and administrative services. . . .

"How did he encourage the heads of those departments to advertise their services to other parts of the company?"

"Did he hold ongoing meetings with his direct reports to encourage them to work together, or did he discourage that kind of intermingling?"

"Did he involve his people in the financials of the organization at all and expect them to take on an ownership mentality, or was that strictly his domain?"

"Should I expect him to be very proactive at coordinating the activities of the various departments he'll oversee at this firm if I bring him aboard, or will he keep the functional areas fairly separate?"

With answers like these factoring into your employment decision, you should be feeling much more confident about the kind of human being you're considering and his projected impact on your existing staff.

84. Please address the candidate's ability to cope with the significant pressures associated with senior management.

Why Ask This Question?

Some people have tendencies toward self-doubt as pressure increases. Others are more likely to overreact to relatively minor setbacks, irritants, and disappointments. Still others are inclined to be run ragged and get burned out when the heat's on. Determining whether candidates are capable of coping with the pressures and rejection involved in senior management tasks necessarily belongs in the reference-checking realm. After all, no candidate will reveal such self-admitted shortcomings in a face-to-face interview.

Analyzing the Response

How to Get More Mileage Out of the Question. This question is broad enough to allow for liberal interpretations. Therefore, you could simply employ this direct query and then allow the former supervisor to fill in the silence and respond. On the other hand, you might want to employ some "trailer" queries to provide the respondent with more concrete choices. Here are some options to follow up the initial question in your reference-checking conversation:

"Would you say that Laura has tendencies toward self-doubt as the pressure increases and the heat's on?"

"Could Laura be accused of being likely to overreact to relatively minor setbacks, irritants, and disappointments?"

"Is she inclined to be run ragged by demanding customers? Similarly, could she be accused of carrying the virtue of a service-minded, helpful attitude past the point of diminishing returns?"

These follow-ups will allow you to articulate the nature of your concerns and help the respondent answer your question more accurately.

85. Does this person ever delay the inevitable in terms of disciplining or dismissing employees?

Why Ask This Question?

Some people just aren't natural-born disciplinarians. As a matter of fact, they'll avoid confrontation whenever possible. Of course, very few managers (as opposed to boxers) enjoy interpersonal conflict. Still, occasionally "nipping at the heels" of underperforming staff members remains a necessary managerial skill. As a matter of fact, it is often said that a CEO's ability to instill fear in his subordinates is one of the most critical elements of executive management. Employing this query as a litmus test of the individual's willingness to set and enforce competitive standards should reveal an important aspect of the candidate's interpersonal and communication skills.

Analyzing the Response

How to Get More Mileage Out of the Question. The previous employer's response must be qualified during the reference check to address under what circumstances the candidate will formally discipline or terminate a direct report. In addition to determining what triggers the candidate's call to action, you also have to uncover whether the candidate confronts subordinates in a constructive or negative fashion.

A practical way to generate details regarding the candidate's natural inclination to discipline underperformers is to apply a fictitious comparison—in other words, you would state what problems the last manager had (which may be exaggerated for the purpose of amplifying this issue), and then ask the former employer to measure the candidate against this fictitious past manager's performance. For example, you might state:

> "Mary, our last vice-president of sales probably failed to discipline underperformers as she should have, and too many branches weren't reaching their potential because a number of the branch managers took advantage of her good nature and her unwillingness to address problems. . . .

> "What kinds of turnover patterns did you notice when Peter was at the helm of national sales in your company?"

> "What typically triggered his need to formally discipline or terminate someone?"

> "When he needed to be a disciplinarian, did you find his approach to be open and constructive or aggressive and caustic?"

"What was the most common cause of termination during his tenure?"

"Could he ever be accused of being so reluctant to engage in a confrontation that his managerial effectiveness suffered?"

Again, painting a picture of a nonassertive supervisor against which the candidate can be measured will help you clarify the candidate's past performance in one of the most challenging areas of interpersonal communications: direct discipline.

86. Is this individual inclined to maintain smooth and amicable relations at all costs, or is she more likely to show her teeth when faced with adversity?

Why Ask This Question?

On a broader basis, this query continues the theme of the previous one. Unlike the former question, however, it addresses the candidate's dealings with peers and superiors as opposed to subordinates. If you're not comfortable with the answer you get in the last question and want more evidence of this individual's ability to manage problem situations aggressively and gear up for interpersonal conflict, then pose this follow-up query to develop the issue further.

Analyzing the Response

Simply put, if this query reveals someone incapable of or unwilling to meet a challenging coworker head-on, then this issue could very well function as a negative swing factor in the final selection process. Few hires require the talents of a strict disciplinarian, but a nonengaging communication style coupled with an unstructured supervisory approach could leave subordinates without a proper sense of direction or desired level of accountability. Such individual shortcomings could lead to a swift breakdown in productivity.

87. Does the candidate stay open to all sides of an argument before reaching a decision, or does he get personally involved in conflicts?

Why Ask This Question?

What if the preceding question generates a response showing that the candidate may be all too swift to dismiss a subordinate or aggressively show his teeth when faced with conflict? It's simply not practical to ask a past employer about the candidate's argumentative nature. Questions like "Is Peter apt to indulge in argument for argument's sake?" or "Is Peter unduly concerned about who is right rather than what is right?" could appear to attack the candidate unfairly and force the past employer to defend the candidate's actions.

Still, insensitivity in the executive suite could result in more than just hurt feelings and an angst-ridden staff. Verbal and sexual harassment, wrongful termination, and discrimination charges often occur when one manager is too liberal about his personal feelings or lacks sensitivity and awareness of others' personal rights. You can't afford to add a "Bloody Mary" to your staff in today's overly litigious employee rights environment. And you certainly don't want to be in a position to have to temper a senior manager's impulsive inclinations in such a delicate area.

Analyzing the Response

How to Get More Mileage Out of the Question. Assuming that the past employer admits that she's seen Peter take more of a personal stance in certain circumstances than was probably appropriate, you should logically follow up with:

> "Give me an example of a time when he prematurely reached a conclusion without having all the necessary details. How could he cultivate a greater sense of objectivity at this point in his career? Is it simply his style to shoot from the hip? Does his defensiveness stem from insecurity? Does he rule by intimidation and prefer to kick up all the dust so that he maintains control of the situation? Or is he just naturally a more abrasive and antagonistic person?"

Such queries will no doubt unearth fairly negative examples of the individual's propensity to attack others or overzealously defend himself. Once again, though, being forewarned is forearmed because such information will put you in a better position for damage control once the inevitable surfaces—if you decide to hire such a candidate despite his weaknesses in this area.

Sixteen

Preempting the Counteroffer: Steering Candidates Clear of Temptation

Counteroffers are simply enticements to keep employees aboard once they have given notice. Employers have historically been known to appeal to a departing worker's sense of loyalty, guilt, or fear to convince individuals to change their minds about resigning. It is not even uncommon to hear of offers of promotions, huge salary increases, and spousal perks to entice resigning employees to reject a new employer's offer.

It probably seems more logical to handle counteroffer issues with candidates *after* they've accepted your job offer. After all, most employers reason that they have to offer someone a job before the candidate will receive a counteroffer. However, it's critical to address counteroffer issues *before* extending an employment offer. Once you make an employment offer, you give total control over to the candidate. The individual then could very well use the counteroffer threat as leverage to negotiate more money from you. Remember, the counteroffer is just another variable in the employment process that you need to control.

What should you do if a candidate intimates that he'll consider a counteroffer from his present employer? Simply advise him to address his needs with his boss right now: "Joe, why don't you go back and speak with your department head about your needs before we go any further? If you get the extra money that you're looking for, then you'll have to agree that my suggestion was good for your career. On the other hand, if you don't get the added compensation that you're looking for, then call me back and I'll address our offer a little more seriously. . . ." Excellent work! You have proactively removed an arrow from the candidate's quiver that could have come back to hurt you later in the negotiation process.

Making employees counteroffers once they've given notice is a poor management practice. The strongest companies avoid subjecting themselves to counteroffer coercion. That's primarily because this strategy typically fails to solve the problems that made the employee want to leave in the first place. Statistically speaking, many companies that make counteroffers to resigning employees have experienced that counteroffers serve only to delay the inevitable: In a large percentage of cases, workers who accept counteroffers are gone within six months anyway. Indeed, keeping disgruntled workers aboard only hurts an employer's chances of shoring up weaknesses in the organization and making the necessary changes to move successfully into the future.

Besides, subjecting oneself to counteroffer coercion sends the wrong message to existing staff; throwing dollars at people to stay aboard once they've obviously shown themselves to be disloyal is a desperate move on the company's part and poor career management on the individual's part. In short, very little good has historically come to either party from accepted counteroffers.

In contrast, companies that respect their employees' freedom to accept other employment offers send the right message to their remaining staff. The manager wishes the individual well and then swiftly joins forces with existing workers to redesignate the current workload and fill the opening quickly. Employees leave those organizations with a minimum of friction and histrionics. No feelings are hurt, no undue pressure is exerted, and the corporate family has the chance to work together to rebuild from the loss.

This chapter will address counteroffer issues from a "resignation drill" perspective. Although you know how dangerous it is for individuals to accept counteroffers, and even though your company may steer away from such practices, that doesn't mean that the candidate you're courting right now won't be subjected to counteroffer pressures once she returns to her office to give notice.

Resignation drills occur very often in the recruitment industry when headhunters take their candidates through role-play scenarios of giving notice to the current boss. It makes sense for recruiters to spend some time preparing the candidate to resign so as to avoid surprises at the finish line that could wipe out all the work that's gone into the negotiations up to that point. So it's practical business sense that leads recruiters down this path. Resignation drills will benefit you as well as the hiring manager by dramatically increasing the chances that candidates will accept your employment offer and make a clean break from their current companies.

88. Tell me again why you feel the position you're applying for meets your career needs or why working for our company is so important for you.

Why Ask This Question?

Once you've concluded all rounds of face-to-face interviews, thoroughly checked a candidate's references, and administered various tests and assessment tools, it's time to mentally prepare the candidate to accept your offer. The counteroffer "prep" and resignation drill function as a preclosing technique to ensure that the candidate is aware that he will be "propositioned" once he returns to his current office to give notice. Therefore, the initial step in the process will require that the candidate voices out loud what benefits he'll gain by joining your company. This is specifically done by focusing him on how his personal or career needs are linked to the opportunity that your organization offers.

Analyzing the Response

Candidates typically join companies for one of three reasons. They are motivated either because of:

1. The company and its growth plans, market niche, high-profile name-brand recognition, or reputation as a quality employer.
2. The position's variety, pace, opportunity for self-expression, reporting relationship, or scope of authority.
3. The people they met along with the way in the interview process who gave them the feeling that they would fit in, be appreciated, and be recognized for their contributions.

Inviting candidates to reiterate what is most important to them serves as the foundation for going forward with the offer. Candidates must convince you and themselves that their reason for leaving their present position won't come up again in the foreseeable future at your company. Don't assume that the benefits and the appeal of your organization are obvious to an outsider.

89. On a scale of 1 to 10 (10 being you're really excited about accepting our offer, 1 being there's no interest), where do you stand?

Why Ask This Question?

If the previous query openly invites candidates to articulate their understanding of the benefits your organization has to offer them from a personal or career standpoint, then this follow-up query concretely qualifies their interest level. It forces candidates to come to terms with their own emotions and motives for job change as well as to volunteer any concerns they have about accepting your offer.

Analyzing the Response

This "1 to 10" question is an absolute litmus test for gauging an individual's emotional state. If you ask the candidate where she falls on a scale of 1 to 10, and she responds that she's an absolute 10, that's great! But beware: These are relative numbers, and it's the reasoning behind the numbers that counts, not the numbers themselves. For example, if Laura says that she's a 10, your immediate comeback is, "Well, that's excellent, Laura. I'm happy to hear that. What makes you a 10?"

Good Answers. By qualifying the number, the candidate is forced to articulate her definition of a 10. If Laura is a 10 because she's currently a management consultant for a Big 6 accounting firm who wants to move into a client company for her first controllership, then your offer makes solid business sense for both of you. The chances of her rejecting this offer are slim.

RED FLAGS. If, on the other hand, she's a 10 because she's having difficulties getting along with her fickle boss, then she may be a "fake 10." Interpersonal relationships change quickly with erratic superiors, so that one day you're in and the next day you're out. Consequently, if the two "kiss and make up," so to speak, or that boss leaves the company, then your "motivated 10" candidate might succumb to a counteroffer anyway. Beware the jilted subordinate.

How to Get More Mileage Out of the Question. Let's say, however, that Laura answers that she's an 8. In that case, you need a threefold comeback:

1. "Why are you an 8?"
2. "What would make you a 10?" And then,
3. "If that issue could be resolved, where would you then rank on a scale of 1 to 10?"

The key to this discussion obviously lies in closing the gap between the individual's perception of your opportunity and the reality of the job you're offering. Then it's simply a matter of confirming that no other roadblocks are in the way that could hinder the individual from accepting your offer. Here's how this scenario plays itself out:

You: Laura, why do you consider yourself an 8?

Candidate: Well, after doing my research, I really feel that a controllership in a company of this size should pay no less than $80,000. Your offer of $65,000 is somewhat less than I expected. I appreciate the fact that you're limited by internal equity in that you can't pay me more than your existing staff members who hold similar levels of responsibility. Still, we really didn't discuss salary until yesterday, and although I'm extremely interested in joining your company, I was somewhat disappointed because I feel you're paying below the market.

You: Okay, what would your compensation package look like to make you a 10?

Candidate: First, I'm currently earning $72,000 as a senior consultant, so I'd like a base of no less than that. On the other hand, if you really can't offer more than $65,000 in base salary, I'd like to receive a sign-on bonus that brings me to $72,000 and an options package that exceeds the base. . . .

You: I can't commit to you, Laura, that we could come up with a sign-on bonus or offer you the options you're requesting. I need to put a pencil to paper first. Now that I know what your expectations are, though, I have something concrete to work with. Let's put this issue aside for a moment. Assuming that I can create a compensation package that meets your needs, then where would you rank on a scale of 1 to 10?

Candidate: I'd be an absolute 10 and would be ready to join ranks by the middle of next month.

Notice how you've skillfully helped the candidate flesh out her arbitrary 8 rating on the interest scale. You isolated her objection and then probed for other areas that concerned her. Finally, you preclosed her to accept your offer if her conditions were met. Voilà—you made a skillful employment offer that considered her needs and attempted to resolve her concerns before asking her to commit to you. Such practices will build goodwill in the preemployment process and convince new hires that your company sets people up to win by putting others' needs first.

90. What would have to change at your present position for you to continue working there?

Why Ask This Question?

Whenever you're dealing with someone who's doing excellent work for a competing company, it is safest to spend some time analyzing what's going on in the person's current position so that you understand how your offer stacks up against it. Of course, if a candidate is currently unemployed, this question has no application.

Analyzing the Response

Probably 70 percent of corporate Americans who willingly change jobs do so not because of technical matters but because of interpersonal conflict. When polled in survey after survey, American workers rank recognition first among their top work priorities. This is usually followed by other emotional factors like enjoyable work and the ability to contribute to the team. Surprisingly, salary usually ranks fourth on the charts of reasons why employees stay with or leave a company! If recognition for a job well done ranks first, and it has direct linkage to interpersonal relationships with coworkers (and especially direct supervisors), then examining the level of recognition the individual currently receives is an important factor in the preemployment offer process.

Good Answers. When employing this query, look first for responses that are out of the individual's control. Pending layoffs, corporate relocations, and overall job insecurity will often result in the candidate responding, "Paul, nothing could change at my present company to entice me to stay." That points to a clean break with the current employer and a graceful transition into your firm.

Red Flags. In contrast, if the candidate responds vaguely, "Well, I can't really think of anything that could change at my present company and convince me to stay," then challenge her further by stating:

"I've found that one or two changes could often make an individual think twice about leaving a company. What would those one or two areas be in your case?"

If that query still only generates a superficial or vague response, probe even deeper:

"Tell me, Laura, about the recognition you get for a job well done. Do you feel that your contribution is properly recognized, or is it somehow diminished by your current supervisor?"

You're obviously leading the candidate down the path of coworker relationships. For the noncommittal candidate who is reluctant to address shortcomings about her present company lest she weaken her negotiation posture, or for someone who hasn't given much thought to fixing relationship problems back at the office, this questioning pattern should force a critical issue to a head. After all, there's very likely a weak link somewhere in the chain that binds the candidate to her present company, and statistically there's an excellent chance that it stems from a people problem.

Even if the candidate feels that she's properly recognized for her efforts, this add-on query regarding the individual's relationship with her boss will naturally segue into other reasons for leaving:

"No, my relationship with my boss is fine. It's just that the company lacks state-of-the-art systems that would allow me to stay on top of the power curve in my field. Also, they brought in a new CEO about four months ago who's really changed the way things are done back at the office. All in all, I feel it's the right time for me to explore other career options. So there's really nothing that could change that would motivate me to stay."

Bravo! You've brought this issue to a logical conclusion and mandated that the candidate voice out loud that the situation is most likely beyond repair. That's an important psychological step to prepare the person to make the break. It also allows you to further understand how you should position your offer once the time comes.

91. Tell me about the counteroffer they'll make you once you give notice. If you gave notice to your boss right now, what would he say to keep you?

Why Ask This Question?

Ah, this is the heart of the resignation drill—no more beating around the bush! Our first queries in this session were roundabout probes to gently test for salient career issues that were pushing candidates out of their present companies' arms or, inversely, that could lead to counteroffer acceptance. This query mentally prepares the individual to deal with the counteroffer awaiting her. This way, when it comes, it won't be a surprise that catches the candidate off guard or otherwise lets her emotions cloud her better business judgment.

If, on the other hand, the company makes no counteroffer, then the candidate (who, because of your prompting, is preparing for one) may feel disappointed that she wasn't pursued more aggressively to stay aboard. Such an emotion will only enforce her conclusion that accepting your offer was the right thing to do all along. In either situation, your preclosing drill will have set the stage for a smooth transition out of her present company and into the new environment.

Analyzing the Response

Preparing for a concrete challenge to your potential offer makes practical sense and allows you to take sides with that individual by working together to plan her resignation and her successful exit out of her current company. A psychological "good guy–bad guy" contrast forms in the candidate's mind with the current boss playing the potential "bad guy" who is out to tempt her with perks that will only stand in the way of her succeeding at a new opportunity. Forewarned is forearmed for candidates too, and this brief exercise removes a snare that could entrap them.

RED FLAGS. If you sense some danger in the candidate's response revealing that a hefty counteroffer will be made or that it will be very hard for the individual to break the personal ties to her boss, follow this query up with an add-on corollary: "What would change on your present position if you *did* accept a counteroffer? Would life six months down the road be any different than it is right now? Would you excel there as you could here?"

By allowing the candidate to play out this scenario in her head, you'll take her past the immediacy of the counteroffer resignation and farther into the future. You know that statistics bear out a bleak reality for those who accept counteroffers, but you can't necessarily say that to the candidate because you're a biased party in this negotiation. However, by pointing the candidate in this future direction, you're allowing her to reach the same conclusions about the limitations of staying with the current employer.

The bottom line to all this is that, as a prospective employer, you are perfectly within your rights to find out what could entice the individual to stay aboard with her current firm. That's not being nosy; it's an effective business offense to gauge a candidate's interest level. After all, you have the job opportunity to offer. No matter how tight the labor market or how specialized a candidate's skills, one law will always remain firm in the land of employment hiring: The employer makes the calls. Use that guaranteed leverage to drill finalist candidates regarding their interest level in your company, their potential to accept a counteroffer, and their overall desire to make a positive impact on your organization. You'll simultaneously help them avoid becoming victim to the dangerous counteroffer syndrome.

Seventeen

Making the Offer and Closing the Deal: Questions to Ensure That Candidates Accept Your Job Offers

Once the interviewing process is completed, candidates should be pre-closed on wanting to accept your job offer. Whether that's because you brought them through a questioning drill that helped them identify their own needs and tie their motives to your company's future or because you framed a real-life scenario of the limitations at their present company after their counteroffer acceptance, candidates should be much more receptive. After all, the worst time for them to be examining the pros and cons of leaving one company and joining another is now—at the actual time of the offer. Emotions run high at the finish line, and if they haven't played out this final scenario in their minds up until now, then they may fall victim to counteroffer temptation.

Of course, your job is not to coddle a candidate. As the employer, you don't want to have to convince someone to come to work for you. After all, if it's that much of a challenge just to get the prospective new hire to say yes to an offer, then this is probably a premature decision on the individual's part. Recall as well that the first decision you watch a candidate make is the acceptance or rejection of your offer. If the offer is accepted only half-heartedly, that may put a damper on this relationship's new beginnings.

Still, don't underestimate the tremendous pressure that most people feel while undergoing this significant rite of passage. In case it's been a while since you yourself changed jobs, think back to the fears you experienced before saying yes to a new start date and goodbye to close friends at your last company. Remember that job change ranks right up there with fear of public speaking and fear of death in terms of causing anxiety in most of us humans. And rightfully so—severing the ties with a job where you know exactly what's expected of you, with your corporate family, the familiar restaurants where you have lunch, and the comfortable chair that you've broken in to fit your back conjures up intense fears in even the most confident people:

> "What if the grass isn't greener on the other side? What if the new company experiences an unforeseen layoff? At least here I've got tenure and would probably survive the first few rounds of cuts. I've heard a lot about people getting axed because of the LIFO rule: 'Last in, first out' means that I'd be the first one out on the street. Is my present job really so bad? I mean, at least I like the people and know where I stand. . . . Help, I'm having buyer's remorse!"

Which all points to the significance of making offers softly and delicately. Empathy for the job changer in the final decision process is crucial because while the new opportunity is exciting on the one hand, it requires disloyalty to the current employer on the other. Saying yes to you means simultaneously rejecting the family and friends back at the office. And no matter how much the candidate wants out, emotional twangs of fear and guilt remain. If you therefore approach the final offer (as in the counteroffer role-play) from a "pull" sell rather than a "push" sell standpoint, you'll end up asking questions to make the candidate pursue you rather than vice versa.

The scenario is this: After conducting numerous rounds of interviews with multiple candidates, you boiled down your selection to two people. Both passed muster with everyone involved in the hiring process, both had solid references and test scores, and both were taken through a "resignation drill" as outlined in Chapter 16 to ensure that they would accept your offer. You haven't spoken for two days while you've been deciding which candidate made the final cut. You're now about to make the offer to your primary candidate (of course, you're holding onto candidate 2 just in case candidate 1 balks at the offer), and here's what it sounds like:

92. What's changed since the last time we spoke?

Why Ask This Question?

Simply stated, you should begin the candidate closing process with an assumption that if all the ingredients are there now that were there during the counteroffer role-play, then the candidate should accept your offer. If there is a change in plans on the candidate's part, now's his opportunity to share that with you. Again, the last thing you want to do is jump the gun and make an offer only to have it put on hold because of unforeseen circumstances. Controlling the offer process is, after all, the first thing that a candidate watches *you* do.

Analyzing the Response

Nine times out of ten, the candidate will respond that nothing has changed. In that case, you've got the green light to move forward. And again, you'll have preclosed the individual via this conditioning process that you've been taking him through since your counteroffer drill.

On the other hand, if something has changed, like a sudden increase in responsibilities at the present company, a significant raise, or another job offer, or if the idea of relocating suddenly loses its appeal, then you're pushed back a step to the information-gathering stage that occurs in the counteroffer role-play. Find out what's changed, where the candidate stands on a scale of 1 to 10 in terms of his interest in the position (see Question 89 in Chapter 16), and then go back to the drawing board to see if there's anything you could offer to fix the problem.

RED FLAGS. Beware candidates who suddenly request long time frames to come to a decision. Ideally, the candidate will have had enough opportunity during the multiple rounds of interviews to research your organization, speak with the key players in his area, and determine what your performance expectations are. As a matter of fact, the resignation drill purposely surfaces questionable issues so that these last-minute delay tactics are avoided. Of course, there may be a legitimate reason why a candidate needs an additional twenty-four hours to determine his course of action. But asking for more than twenty-four hours is unacceptable.

That's because candidates who request an additional week or more are usually waiting to hear from a different company about another offer! Putting you off is the only way to buy time to see whether they can generate the offer they really want. This is unfortunate timing for you because you're the backup job offer. If that doesn't hurt your feelings enough, keep in mind that, statistically, the chance of having your offer accepted, even if the individual's primary job doesn't come through, is marginal at best. People who tie their hopes to one job that ends up falling through usually decline the secondary job offer! That's simply human nature: Job 2 most likely won't ever amount to the lost opportunities offered by job 1, reasons the candidate, so he passes on both.

How to Get More Mileage Out of the Question. If you suspect that a candidate is stonewalling you in an attempt to wait for another offer, then communicate your perceptions openly:

> "Dennis, I've found that people who suddenly need more time at the finish line typically haven't gathered enough data to make an informed decision. What's holding you back from saying yes to our offer?"

If you get a vague response, probe further:

> "Dennis, I want to start our relationship on the right foot, and I'd appreciate a candid response. My bet is you've got another offer on the table that might have more appeal to you than ours. If that's the case, I understand. Still, I'd like to know where we stand relative to your other offer."

At that point, if your perceptions are correct, the candidate will admire your intuition and respond to your legitimate concerns. You'll learn what your chances are of landing this individual, and you can prepare either to wait out his decision or to line up other candidates.

Caution. What you don't want to do is attempt to convince the candidate at the finish line that your offer is superior. His focus is definitely on the other offer—otherwise you would have heard an "I'll accept!" already. So persuading him that you're better than his other suitor puts you at a disadvantage in the negotiation process: It will appear that you're begging as you shoot down the other company or try to resell your own. Again, by now you've done all the selling you have to. Make a firm commitment to your own plan of action, and respect the individual's right to plan his own destiny.

93. If you had to choose among three factors—(1) the company, (2) the position you're applying for, or (3) the people you'd be working with—which would you say plays the most significant role in your decision to accept our offer?

Why Ask This Question?

This smacks of an exercise in the counteroffer drill (see question 88 in Chapter 16)—namely, asking candidates to confirm why joining your company makes sense for them from a career or personal standpoint. It bears repetition because when time passes between the interviewing stage and the final offer, it becomes critical to invite the candidate to redefine the benefits of joining your company—both for you and for him. You want to make sure that this candidate has a clear understanding of what your organization is all about; he needs to hear again *out loud* what benefits and opportunities exist by joining your firm.

Analyzing the Response

Good Answers. You'll find that most people choose option 1—the company—as the key reason why they change jobs. People look for the emotional recognition of a job well done; they want to work for a company that takes care of its people; and they want to know that they can make a difference. Those emotional criteria are inherently found in the company and all of its manifestations: its people, corporate culture, and its ambience.

Don't be surprised, however, to find administrative support candidates linking themselves to option three. Workers who define themselves by the relationships they keep often see themselves via the people they report to. So an executive secretary reporting to a chief operating officer will probably base more of her decision to accept your offer on the perceived relationship with the COO.

Similarly, some aggressive corporate ladder climbers may be more motivated by the increased responsibilities that the new position offers. The enticement of a greater span of control, budget, or exposure to new areas of interest increases the individual's overall marketability. Such enticements lock the candidate into accepting the offer.

94. If we were to make you an offer, tell me ideally when you'd like to start. How much notice would you need to give your present employer?

Why Ask This Question?

Notice the use of the subjunctive case in phrasing this statement—"*if we were to make* you an offer. . . .*"* Even though you're about to make an offer within two or three minutes, there's no need to give away the farm. Keeping the candidate at arm's length only serves to heighten the individual's desire and to reinforce your control.

Analyzing the Response

Most candidates will need to give their current employers two weeks' notice. Of course, senior-level managers may need to give several months' notice because of their broad responsibilities and the impact that leaving the company will have. Therefore, the first rule is: Don't pressure candidates to start tomorrow when they have to give appropriate notice. You could build a lot of resentment if you force individuals to walk away from their present company without giving that organization ample time to locate and train a replacement.

High performers are sophisticated consumers regarding the employment marketplace, and they realize that their current employers will be providing reference-check information about them for the next ten years. No one wants to risk a negative future reference saying, "Oh, Doris was a solid performer, but she left us without notice. That really stuck in my throat and was a very disappointing end to an otherwise excellent track record." In short, if you need someone immediately, hire a temp. But let candidates determine their own timeliness for giving notice (as long as it's a reasonable amount of time for the amount of responsibility that they hold).

RED FLAGS. The second rule is: Watch out for people who don't feel obligated to give their current employers any notice. After all, you don't expect to be left high and dry when this person decides to move on to greener pastures. More importantly, the decision to leave a company without giving any notice reveals little loyalty or character.

Consequently, the person's inclination to follow proper corporate etiquette may in itself play a role in your decision to extend the offer! Remember, you still haven't offered the job yet, and it's not too late to put the individual on hold, catch your breath, and then promise to call back later. Buying yourself some extra time at this point is perfectly acceptable.

95. Share with me what final questions I can answer for you to help you come to an informed career decision.

Why Ask This Question?

This is the final setup before the salary negotiation. It gives you a chance to show yourself as a concerned and empathetic future employer. Such consideration will no doubt be very welcome to all candidates about to make a break with one company and a commitment to another. As such, this benevolent posturing should be assumed in all final negotiations. More importantly, it invites any issues or concerns that could botch the acceptance of the offer.

Analyzing the Response

If any issues other than salary beg for more consideration on the candidate's part, then go back to the drawing board and handle those concerns first before moving on to the final and most critical element of all—making the salary offer.

Candidates will typically ask for confirmations about the job responsibilities, reporting relationships, or benefits packages. Sometimes they'll mention that they've got a four-day holiday already planned that can't be canceled. Maybe they'll need to give three weeks' notice instead of two. Now's the time for such "incidentals" to surface.

CAUTION. What shouldn't occur, though, is that candidates' demands suddenly skyrocket. For example, if an individual states that he forgot to tell you that he has $15,000 worth of stock options that he expects you to include in his base salary, that smacks of extortion. Such "take it or leave it" propositions at the finish line are the ultimate show of poor negotiation timing. Be very leery of going ahead with an offer when such "leveraging" occurs in the eleventh hour.

96. At what dollar level would you accept our job offer, and at what dollar level would you reject it?

Why Ask This Question?

Well, if this isn't the $64,000 question! This is probably the most critical query in the entire employment process . . . and in this book!

Why so? Because this is the first time that you give all the power to the candidate. Up to this point, you've maintained control of the entire process: You've carefully guided the candidate and paced her through the interviewing process. You've preclosed her on accepting your offer during the counteroffer drill. And you've shown yourself to be a caring employer by bending over backward to address any questions or doubts so that the individual could come to an informed career decision.

And now comes the showstopper. You've opened the curtain, and after the wonderful presentation you've done regarding the *potential* behind that curtain, the candidate finally comes face to face with the prize. So if she doesn't like it, it's all over. Still, you want to maintain as much control of this business negotiation as possible. Therefore, you phrase your question very carefully. . . .

The key to the question lies in its tag: ". . . at what dollar level would you reject [the offer]?" The reasoning, quite logically, is that this particular phraseology poses a fear of loss. It is exactly that fear that will keep the candidate from becoming too cocky and unmanageable at the finish line.

You may be thinking at this point:

"Goodness, this is a lot of work to 'massage' a job candidate into accepting an employment offer. I'm in the plastic injection molding business, not the headhunting business. Save this finesse stuff for the headhunters who make their livelihoods in staffing companies or finding people work!"

The appropriate response to your argument is:

"Hold on, there. Like it or not, you are in sales, and selling your company is the first order of the day. Furthermore, bending over backward to allay any candidate's concerns will only increase your reputation as a quality employer. And despite having emerged in the early 1990s from the largest economic contraction since the Great Depression, finding qualified people is hard work! Therefore, you owe it to yourself to spend extra time at the finish line. Don't let weeks of work and recruitment expenses be wasted because of your haste in making an offer. Salary negotiations need to be finessed, and it's your responsibility to ensure that the candidate learns that you're putting her needs right alongside your own."

Analyzing the Response

How to Get More Mileage Out of the Question. Let's run through a few common scenarios that have been known to snag even the most well-prepared employers. No doubt you've been caught in one of these situations yourself, so now's the time to give heed to the lessons you've learned.

- *Situation 1: The malleable candidate.* Let's assume you're very straightforward in your classified recruitment advertising or that the individual learned during the interview process that the salary range for technical writers at your company is $3,000 to $3,600 per month. The candidate is currently earning $3,200 per month (pretty much the midpoint of your salary range), and you plan to reward this new hire with a 10 percent increase in base pay.

    When it comes time to make the offer, you explain two things to the candidate in consideration: "First, Christina, I want you to know that we believe in making salary offers that reward new hires with a 10 percent increase in base pay whenever possible; second, please understand that we've got to look at internal equity before making any final decisions. If, for example, a 10 percent increase in base pay would end up paying you more than an existing employee who has more experience, then that 10 percent rule of thumb increase would no longer apply. Does that make sense?"

    The candidate agrees, and the offer continues like this: "Christina, we've taken a look at your years of experience and your performance track record, and we're happy to tell you that we can indeed offer you the 10 percent increase that we were originally planning on. Therefore, we'd like to offer you the position at $3,520 a month." Then Christina shrieks with excitement, accepts your offer, and wonders how she's going to be able to spend $320 more a month from now on!

- *Situation 2: The law of inverse gravity.* Sometimes the story doesn't have such an amicable ending. One of the dangers of letting candidates know the range of the position is that they hear only the top end of the range, while you only want to pay at the bottom of the range. And there you have it: you're upside down in the deal. Should you let candidates know salary ranges in general? Probably not. The extra information will typically do more harm than good. Christina in our former example was very understanding: she realized that just because the position had a maximum potential of $3,600 per month, that didn't mean that she was going to get that amount. She accepted that fact readily.

CAUTION. But what about Denise? When she was made the offer at $3,520 (and she had a very similar employment history to Christina), she felt insulted. "After all, aren't I worth $3,600 per month? Who works harder than I do? If the salary range goes to $3,600 and I'm only being offered $3,520, this company obviously feels that I'm not the best person for the job. I can't believe they're making such a big deal about $80 a month. And if they thoroughly checked my references, they would have realized *how much I'm valued by my current employer.*" Whoops! Now you're the bad guy, and the current employer is the good guy. Not an effective way to make employment offers.

So how do you avoid the law of inverse gravity? Simply by not mentioning ranges to candidates at all. Instead, once you've asked the person what her salary requirements are during the interview, state "This position is in your salary range." This way, no "target" salaries are established and the individual keeps an open mind throughout the negotiations.

Let's take this one step further. What if the candidate already knows the high end of the range despite your efforts to keep it secret? How do you convince this person that $3,520 is a fair offer and that you're not a cheapskate? Well, it does indeed put you at a disadvantage when you have to defend your offer. Still, there is a very commonsense way to objectively explain the reasoning behind your decision. It's called *internal equity.*

Internal equity simply means that employees with like amounts of experience, tenure, and skill sets earn similar rates of pay. It wouldn't make sense to hire a new employee and pay her more than an existing employee who holds the same position unless there were extenuating circumstances (like the new worker having ten years of experience when the existing staff member only has three). Therefore, explain to the candidate:

> "Denise, we don't make salary offers in a vacuum. Although our ranges from low to high for a given position could be very far apart, when it comes down to making the offer, we match the new hire's years of experience, skills, and abilities with the experiences of our existing staff members. Your final salary offer closely matches the salaries of the existing employees to whom you're benchmarked."

Such reasoning is clean, concise, and most importantly, objective. It is absolutely critical that the candidate not perceive that there were any personal issues involved in your decision-making process. This strategy works 95 percent of the time. In situations where it doesn't work, that's because the candidate is unable to look at the issue from an objective distance and realize that the offer is based on valid business fundamentals. Losing that type of candidate at the finish line, however, may bode well for your company in the long run.

- *Situation 3: Making offers for newly created positions when you're not sure how much to pay.* Creating new positions in your company and adding expertise because of the demands of increased business is exciting indeed. Don't feel, though, that you're the only employer who's ever run an ad in the Sunday *Times* without any idea of what that job would be paying. It happens all the time! But what happens when you're down to the finish line, the vice president you're looking at hiring was making $165,000 a year in base salary at her last company but was laid off two years ago and hasn't been able to find work since? In other words, how do you decide how much to offer when all the rules of compensation law fall by the wayside?

    The only solution to such a quagmire is to involve the candidate in the creation of a compensation package. No candidate will shy away from telling you off the cuff how much she should be paid. (It's usually a fairly high number relative to her past salary history!) But by engaging the candidate in developing a compensation plan relative to the position's impact on the corporate bottom line—its reporting relationship, scope of authority in terms of supervision and budgets, and the projected increases in company profitability that will result because of it—you'll get much more objective feedback from someone who probably knows that position's market worth better than anyone at your company.

    Let's take an example. First, you've got to give the candidate some parameters. Your position is paying in the $80,000 to $100,000 range. The candidate knows that coming in to this negotiation. (Note that you should always tell someone the salary range if it's significantly *below* what she has been making. That's only fair since you don't want to waste anyone's time.) She's hungry to jump back into the market after two years on the sidelines, however, and she knows that she won't get the $165,000 base she had at her last company. She also knows that your company has done only retail home equity mortgage lending and that it desperately needs to gain access to the profitable wholesale market. Because she took her last company into wholesale and understands the pressures and pitfalls of developing new business lines, she's exactly what the doctor ordered as far as you're concerned.

    So step 1 sounds like this:

"Dorothy, now that you've studied our annual report, met with all the players in the decision-making process, and understand where we want you to go with this new wholesale product line, I'd like you to map out specific details regarding your expected base salary, bonus, options, perks, or whatever else is important to you. Bear in mind what our original salary range is, then make a case for your specific package. Fax me an acceptable compensation package for your first two years so that I can bring it to our senior management committee."

In explaining that this compensation proposal will be shared with the board of directors or executive committee, there is a lesser chance of exaggerated demands. Further, sometimes executives will be fairly flexible in terms of base salary requirements when other nonmonetary or deferred compensation issues could instead be added. It never hurts to ask, and you may learn of noncash perks that the person values at this point in her life that could cost you little in terms of up-front cash and gain you lots of negotiation leverage.

The candidate's proposal looks like this:

Base Salary	Bonus	Options	Total Comp.
Year 1 $100,000	10% first year	1000 options @ $50 each	$160,000
Year 2 $105,000	20% second year	1000 options @ $50 each	$176,000

In making this proposal, the candidate has set out to put a substantial portion of her pay at risk. After all, bonuses are discretionary on the basis of corporate and individual performance, and options may expire worthless if not exercised. So in terms of pure payroll output, this individual is within your range.

Armed with the parameters that would make this candidate happy, you then have the option of perhaps cutting 10 percent off the first year base but increasing the number of awardable options at the end of the second year. Whatever your final allocation, you're not shooting in the dark! Without this candidate's road map, you risk personally alienating the individual by making an insulting offer. Worse, you run the risk of coming off as a naive employer because you're not familiar with whole-sale compensation practices. On the upside, you may occasionally learn that certain noncash rewards carry a lot of weight in a candidate's mind, and that only helps to keep your payroll expenses down.

Therefore, involve the new hire in every aspect of the compensation plan creation. Few things in corporate America will work as well to build a shared sense of openness in information sharing, a greater sense of part-nership, and increased accountability.

PART III

Key Interviewing and Reference-Checking Issues

Eighteen

Staying Within the Law: Interview Questions to Avoid at All Costs!

No book on interviewing questioning techniques would be complete without an acknowledgment that certain queries could land you in hot water legally. You could get into trouble for the illegal use of the non-job-related information that you obtained by asking a query in the preoffer stage of the hiring process. If a candidate believes that she was discriminated against because of improper information that you uncovered during the interview, for example, then that individual could bring suit against you for failing to hire her. The cost of *defending* such claims could be significant in terms of your company's monetary and time investments. The penalties for *losing* the suit itself typically include wages the applicant would have earned if hired plus the individual's attorney's fees. The average cost of a lost employment suit, win or lose, can exceed $100,000.

How difficult is it to steer clear of legal snares? Fortunately not too difficult, especially if your staff is adequately trained and armed with the following information. As a matter of fact, with the number of people interviewing candidates in your company at any given time who could potentially be exposing your organization to unnecessary litigation, this section of the book might well become a critical training module for your newly hired managers.

Although no one aims to blatantly transgress federal or state guidelines that bar various forms of discrimination, the intent is not at issue: only the form of the hiring manager's questions. So let's briefly take a look at some of the more common unacceptable preemployment inquiries that are floating around out there.

Inappropriate Question 1: "What's your maiden name so that I can check your references?"

Asking for a female's maiden name can discriminate against her on the basis of marital status and possibly national origin. Instead, ask whether the candidate has used any other names in the past (not necessarily due to marriage) that will allow your company to verify the person's past work experience and education.

Inappropriate Question 2: "How old are you? What year were you born? When did you graduate from high school?"

State and federal law protects those over forty years old. It promotes the hiring, promotion, and other terms and conditions of employment of older people based upon their abilities rather than their age. There's no problem questioning the year of college graduation because people can graduate from college at any time in their lives, so there's no way to figure out the person's age. But nearly all high schoolers graduate at seventeen or eighteen, so an individual's year of birth could readily be determined by subtracting eighteen from the year of graduation. That's why asking for high school graduation dates must be avoided.

That might raise another issue in your mind, though. Are you still liable for information (written or spoken) volunteered by a candidate without your prompting? Yes! So to defend yourself, you've got to remove anything written on an employment application that could compromise your adherence to proper interviewing guidelines. When a candidate mentions something out loud that doesn't belong in your meeting (for example, "I'm forty-seven years old," "I'm so excited—I just found out I'm pregnant!" or "I learned to speak English after I moved to America when I was eighteen"), immediately let the person know that such information isn't relevant to the interview. Move on to another issue, and by all means, don't write any of that information down on the employment application, resumé, or even on Post-It notes—all are subject to subpoena in the legal discovery process!

Inappropriate Question 3: "Where were you born? Are you a U.S. citizen? Where did you learn to speak Spanish?"

These questions transgress guidelines regarding national origin, birth-place, and citizenship. Instead you should ask, "Could you, *after employment*, submit verification of your legal right to work in the United States?" Questions regarding a candidate's native language or acquisition of foreign languages in general should be avoided unless such language proficiency is an essential function of the particular job.

By the way, is it legal to discriminate against someone because the person has an accent? No! Courts have held that accents are "immutable characteristics" innately tied to an individual's culture. Accordingly, discriminating against someone on the basis of a foreign accent can land you in hot water. However, be practical. You have the right as an employer not to hire a receptionist who is difficult to understand over the phone because her English is stilted. No jury would fault you for that practical business necessity, so you'd pass the "reasonable person" standard with flying colors. Still, when in doubt, speak with an attorney. An ounce of prevention is worth a pound of cure.

Inappropriate Question 4: "Are you married? Are you planning on having children in the next few years? Can you make adequate provisions for child care?"

Whoops! A big no-no on your part! It's a legitimate concern to wonder whether a potential employee can meet overtime demands or report to work on time. However, you are limited by law to stating such things as the hours, any overtime demands, and company travel expectations and then simply questioning whether candidates would have any reason why they couldn't meet those requirements.

Inappropriate Question 5: "Would your religion prevent you from working weekends?"

Asking such a question discriminates on the basis of religious affiliation. It's just as easy and effective to state: "Weekend and holiday work is required. Is that acceptable to you as a condition of employment?"

Inappropriate Question 6: "Are you disabled? Do you have any previous major medical problems? Have you ever filed for worker's compensation? How many days

were you sick last year? Do you have AIDS? What prescription drugs are you currently taking? Have you ever been treated for alcoholism or mental health problems?"

The Americans with Disabilities Act (ADA) of 1992 requires businesses with fifteen or more employees to make their facilities accessible to the physically and mentally disabled and prohibits job discrimination on the basis of disability. The ADA says that a company can't exclude a qualified person from a job if that individual can perform the "essential functions" of the job either unaided or with "reasonable accommodation." The terms in quotation marks are, of course, subject to legal interpretation. To play it safe, though, all you have to remember to ask after presenting a candidate with an accurate job description is, "Are you capable of performing the position's essential job functions with or without accommodation?"

Inappropriate Question 7: "Have you ever been arrested?"

It is allowable to ask a candidate whether he has ever been convicted of a felony, but this question (typically found on your employment application) must typically be accompanied by a statement that a conviction will not necessarily disqualify the candidate from consideration for the job. If you're wondering what the difference is between being arrested and being convicted of a felony, it's that those arrested are presumed innocent until proven guilty. Moreover, categorically rejecting applicants on the basis of a felony record is a problem for two major reasons. First, the felony may have no relation to the essential functions of the job. Second, such a policy has been held to have an adverse discriminatory impact upon certain ethnic and racial minorities.

Inappropriate Question 8: "What kind of discharge did you get from the military?"

Sorry, folks—military service questions must be limited to relevant skills acquired during service. Period.

Inappropriate Question 9: "Have you ever declared bankruptcy or had your wages garnished?"

There are no acceptable alternative questions that allow you to address these issues before the hire. You are, however, perfectly within your rights to make employment offers contingent upon credit checks provided: (1) applicable state and federal laws are followed; and (2) good credit is necessary to perform the essential functions of the job.

Inappropriate Question 10: "Who is the nearest relative we should contact in case of an emergency?"

It's fine for you to ask for *someone* to contact in case of an emergency. However, asking for the "nearest relative" could border on discrimination by national origin, race, or marital status.

Understand that these protections were set up nationally to level the playing field and give all citizens an equal chance to capitalize on employment opportunities. Seen in the optimistic light in which they were created, these queries help ensure that you (and every other American company) run your business fairly and keep America working. Just so that you don't get the impression that all questions bordering on personal issues are verboten, let's take a brief look at certain personal queries that are allowed under the Americans with Disabilities Act.

Allowable Preemployment Queries Under the ADA

"I see you broke your leg. You must be an avid skier!"

"Can you meet the attendance requirements of this job? How many days did you *take leave* last year?" (Note that the question doesn't say, "How many days were you sick or absent last year?")

"Do you illegally use drugs? Have you used illegal drugs in the past two years?" (The ADA protects recovering alcoholics, but active users of illegal narcotics are certainly not covered under any federal law!)

The bottom line regarding the above preemployment inquiries is that they can indeed discriminate against a candidate's rights to privacy. Although they at first seem somewhat burdensome in terms of hindering your ability to understand a candidate's work habits and reliability, the same issues can usually be found out simply by asking questions a different way (for example, "How many days did you take leave last year?" versus "How many days were you sick?"). In cases where no alternative questions are permissible (for example, military discharge status or credit worthiness), you'll simply have to build a case for the individual's candidacy on other selection criteria. Forcing these forbidden issues tempts fate and simply isn't worth the legal exposure.

Nineteen

Telephone Screening Interviews: Formats and Follow-Ups for Swift Information Gathering

Telephone screening interviews can be a practical defense to the sheer numbers of people applying for jobs these days. Telephone introductions attempt to determine candidate suitability in shorter time frames (roughly ten to fifteen minutes) with less commitment on your part (no courteous small talk or paying for candidate parking). Telephone interviewing skills, in addition, are absolutely essential when setting up interviews across country. With little time in faraway hotels to meet with potential staff for a remote office location, your initial candidate choices become critical. Hence, telephone profiling techniques will help you determine the optimal applicants to select for off-site interviews *before* you fly out of town.

Your strategy for handling telephone interviews, similar to in-person meetings, is twofold: First, employ the following questioning matrix to gather adequate data regarding a candidate's suitability; second, once you've completed your initial questioning strategies, then prepare to sell your company to the candidate. That typically includes forwarding all scheduled candidates an annual report or other company data (or at least pointing out to them a location on-line or in the library where they can research your organization) so that they can familiarize themselves with your firm before the meeting.

The ease of the candidate telephone evaluation will usually be determined by the scope and depth of a person's resumé. The more details, the easier the selection (at least from a technical standpoint). Still, not all candidates are masters at resumé writing, and you obviously don't want to screen out potential high performers because they happened to read an outdated book on resumé development. After all, most job candidates only briefly describe their primary job responsibilities without relating them to the achievements they gained for the company while having carried out those basic duties. Furthermore, most people don't describe their companies' market niches or size as well as their own straight- and dotted-line reporting relationships. That information would obviously make the matching process a lot easier for you, so you'll have to cull it yourself.

There are three major segments of the candidate telephone screen: (1) company and job specifics, (2) candidate's success profile, and (3) assessment of candidate's needs. All three are critical because any one area could knock a candidate out of contention. Furthermore, the information you develop in advance will go a long way toward further preparing for the in-person meeting still to come. Therefore, simply make copies of the matrix and attach it to the resumés (if available) of prospective telephone interviewees. Once you've completed a full round of telephone interviews and gained critical insights into individuals' success profiles and career needs, you'll be better positioned to call back finalists and set up in-person meetings. Note that many of the condensed questions to follow are already profiled elsewhere in the book, so return to the source if you need more detailed explanations for employing each question.

1. Company and Job Information

Information regarding a candidate's job responsibilities, technical orientation, achievement profile, and company market niche will help you quickly determine whether the individual's experience matches your company's brand of doing business. The closer the match between a candidate's present employer (the company's demographics and market specialty) and your firm's operations, the better the chances of a successful hire. The questions in this initial section are more technical and mechanical in nature. As such, they will help you determine a candidate's aptitudes (the "can do" factors) and knowledge (the "know how" factors). Combined with the candidate's emotional needs and motives (the "will do" factors) that follow in the next two sections of the matrix, this telephone questionnaire will provide you with ample information to select qualified individuals for face-to-face interviews.

Company demographics are essential: Question the size of the company in terms of number of employees and amount of annual revenue; distinguish among corporations, partnerships, and sole practitioners; find out how long the company has been in business and where its corporate headquarters are located; distinguish between the number of employees at the candidate's location versus the number of branch offices worldwide; in addition, question the candidate about her branch location's (or division's) ranking compared to other locations. After all, a mediocre performer in the top sales branch in the nation may appeal to you more than a top producer at a branch about to be closed for poor profitability.

Company niche refers to the organization's particular line of business and primary product markets within its industry. For example, all mortgage banking firms sell and service loans. Many, however, specialize in certain areas of the mortgage loan business. Therefore, you might question a candidate over the phone like this: "I can't tell from your resumé exactly where your company made its market:

> "What percentage of your loans were conventional, 'A' loans for borrowers with perfect credit?"

> "What percentage of your loans were for credit-impaired borrowers with subpar histories who required 'B through D' grade paper?"

> "What percentage of your loans were for home purchases versus refinances?"

> "How would you break down your retail from wholesale business operations in terms of revenue production?"

> "How did you develop your business leads? Were you expected to cold-call real estate brokers for their referrals, or were most of the leads incoming from the radio ads you ran?"

Obviously, companies have different ways of carrying on their business operations, and learning about the company's market niche reveals a lot about the expectations that the company had for its employees.

The *progression indicator* (see Question 21 in Chapter 5) asks "Describe how you've progressed through the ranks and landed in your current position at ABC Company." It provides insights into a candidate's assumption of responsibilities beyond the written job description. It is especially useful when evaluating candidates with lots of tenure at a given company who may have made a number of promotional or lateral moves over time. Again, if a candidate has not vertically promoted up the ladder ("Well, Paul, I've been there for six years and have been a programmer analyst the whole time"), then add the follow-up query: "Even though you've held the same position for six years, how have you had to reinvent or redefine your job to meet your company's changing needs?'' (see Question 23 in Chapter 5). This way, you'll gain some quick insights into candidates' penchants for adding value to their companies and motivating themselves.

Salary progression looks for positive earnings progression over time. In today's competitive business environment and corporate America's constantly shifting priorities, it is not uncommon for workers to retool and learn new trades as former skills lose market value. Salary cuts typically go hand in hand with such skill shifts. On the other hand, negative salary progression (meaning that the candidate has made less money each time with the past three or so job changes) could be a warning sign that the individual is incapable of assuming, or unwilling to assume, greater responsibilities. That's because salary and responsibility are inextricably linked. A candidate willing to accept less money often ends up accepting less responsibility, and that could definitely spell career burnout. Proceed with caution and keep questioning until you're comfortable with the individual's explanations for the negative earnings progression.

Direct supervisor(s) and direct report(s) clearly distinguish between straight- and dotted-line reporting relationships. Be sure and clarify both the numbers and titles of subordinates. It's not enough to note that the facilities manager you're speaking with oversees a staff of four people: you've got to identify the roles those subordinates played in the company. For example, supervising two building maintenance technicians and two facilities engineers is different from overseeing four office support clerks.

Technical systems refers to the candidate's software environment. This is essential for information technology professionals in terms of their operating systems experience, software platforms, fourth-generation programming languages, and the like. It is an issue as well for secretaries, staff accountants, and other administrative support staff members.

2. Success Profile

This section of the matrix briefly addresses candidates' awareness of their accomplishments, their motivation for changing jobs, and their inclination to accept a counteroffer from their present employers. (There's no time like the present to preclose the candidate on accepting your job offer if it eventually comes!)

The *greatest accomplishment* query invites candidates to highlight their track records for increasing revenues, decreasing organizational expenses, or saving time. As mentioned earlier in the book, you might prompt a candidate by adding, ''Why is the organization a better place for your having worked there?'' or ''What would a past supervisor say regarding your greatest contribution to the organization?" (See Chapter 2 for some questions along these lines.)

The *reason for leaving* query qualifies the circumstances surrounding the individual's motivation for change. As you know, the reason for leaving represents the link in an individual's career progression. It, more than anything else, helps you understand what drives the candidate's career management strategies. The problem or problems underlying the current reason for leaving must be solved by your organization's programs to ensure a successful transition into your firm.

Counteroffer preparation addresses up front the possibility that the individual will be enticed to stay aboard his current company once he returns to give notice. If the person is employed, it's worth an initial query regarding the likelihood of his being propositioned to stay put. Typical questions you might want to use to probe more deeply include: "What would be your next logical move in progression at your present company?" (See Question 25 in Chapter 5.) "What would have to change at your present position for you to continue working there?" (See Question 95 in Chapter 17.)

3. Assessment of Candidate's Needs

Of all three areas in the telephone screen, this section historically gets the shortest shrift. Yet, because of its emotional nature, it carries the most potential to land a candidate successfully. If the first section determines that the candidate is qualified to do the job and the second section attempts to qualify the individual's motivation for change, then this section helps you determine whether your offer will satisfy individuals—on the basis of their reasons for leaving their current employers.

The two "three criteria" questions for company and position will help you accurately assess the individual's values and long-term goals. Getting a feel for where candidates are currently interviewing can be telling regarding their tastes and expectations. In addition, it helps to sell someone on your company if you happen to know your competitor's strengths and weaknesses.

Remember that most people are more motivated by recognition, challenge, and fulfilling work than they are by money. Therefore, beware the folks who apparently want only higher salaries: They're probably not telling you the whole story. (It's much more often the case that they either feel underrecognized by their bosses for their hard work or sense no opportunity for increased responsibilities at their present position.) Of course, if money is truly the sole motivator, watch out as well: They may be only "recruiter's bait" waiting to leapfrog to a higher-paying position elsewhere.

Pace (see Question 41 in Chapter 8) questions the candidate's desire to work under varying tempos or rhythms—the choices are already outlined for you on the matrix.

Similarly, *management style* (see Question 28 in Chapter 6) refers to the individual's preference for ongoing structure, feedback, and direction versus autonomy and independence. It also addresses the person's inclination to manage others via a participatory supervisory style based on consensus building from below versus a more centralized, closed-fisted style that trickles down to subordinates from above. (See Question 78 in Chapter 15.)

Finally, remember to broach a very critical issue before you fly across country or put a candidate on an airplane to visit you: the *minimum salary requirement*. (See Question 96 in Chapter 17.) This will certainly sound premature since you've neither met yet nor had the chance to discuss other compensation components. Still, telephone interviews are meant to crystallize the entire prequalification process, so it is indeed allowable in this case to surface this very important issue before proceeding any further. You'll find the Telephone Interviewing Matrix on the next page.

Telephone Interviewing Matrix

Candidate's Name: _____

Today's Date: _____

Position Title/Location: _____

Resumé Attached?   Yes _____   No _____

I. Company and Job

- Company demographics (size)
- Company niche (primary product markets, specialty areas)
- Progression indicator ("Describe how you've progressed though the ranks and landed your current position. . . .")
- Salary progression (distinguish base salary from bonuses or commission)
- Direct supervisor(s) (number and titles)
- Direct report(s) (number and titles)
- Technical systems

II. Success Profile

- Greatest accomplishment (increased revenues, decreased costs)
- Reason for leaving (qualify circumstances!)
- Counteroffer preparation ("What's your next logical move in progression at your present company? What would have to change at your present position for you to continue working there?")

III. Assessment of Candidate's Needs

- Three criteria for selecting your next company
- Three criteria for selecting your next position
- Pace you prefer: (a) moderate, controllable, and predictable; (b) fast-paced, deadline pressure; (c) "hyperspace" like the trading floor of the stock exchange
- Management style: structure/feedback/direction versus independence and autonomy; consensus building, participative supervisory style versus centralized, autocratic decision making
- Not to limit you or commit you to a certain dollar figure, but what's the minimum salary you'd consider right now to accept another position?

Close: We've got a few more candidates to speak with over the phone before we set up in-person interviews. Allow me to get back to you by tomorrow night if we're in a position to invite you in for a meeting.

Twenty

Getting Real Information From Reference Checks

It is often said that no matter how skilled the interviewer, interviewing is at best a limited activity with restricted potential to predict on-the-job performance. And I agree that this is perfectly true. While you're at it, you could throw references into the same argument: Past employers rarely share performance problems with you, nor will they reveal patterns of inconsistencies or obstacles that past workers experienced. And don't forget about aptitude tests: Capacity for analytical problem solving has very little bearing on daily performance or "street smarts" gained from the school of hard knocks.

So why don't you just hire whoever happens to walk in the front door? Because experience bears out that taking interview feedback, references, and tests into consideration paints a much more reliable picture of an individual's probable performance on the job. Although no one exercise in the employee selection process can guarantee future work habits, multiple evaluations and assessments will increase the *probability* of locating high-performance individuals whose business and personal styles match your organization's corporate culture.

References are critical elements in the candidate selection process. Unlike interviews, reference checks provide objective, third-party feedback of what it's like working with the candidate on a day-to-day basis. Who better than the individual's past supervisor to comment on strengths, weaknesses, pace, interpersonal communications, and aptitudes? And unlike tests, reference checks have real-world application—they're not just measurements of pure intelligence in a vacuum. Indeed, making employment offers without having spoken to past supervisors is like having a loose cannon on the deck of your ship. Without that human evaluation element, you risk missing the historic dimension of working side by side with the candidate. You also run the risk of getting snared by the "professional interviewer" who interviews much better than he actually performs on the job.

The questions that follow in the next three sections are designed to provide you with critical insights regarding a candidate's historical work performance. Up to now, you've asked interviewees to evaluate themselves in comparison with their peers. You've measured their abilities to reduce operating expenses, save time, and increase the work flow. You've gauged their understanding of how their jobs met their departments' key strategic objectives and what roles their departments played in making their prior companies successful. And you've consistently employed behavior-based interviewing questions to ensure that candidates put their initial responses into a real-world context, thereby avoiding canned, superficial answers.

Still, you have only a one-sided argument until you bounce your findings off of the other key player who has the ability to confirm the information you've developed: the candidate's immediate past supervisor. This individual is the only person in the universe capable of verifying your insights into this prospective new hire's ability to make an impact on your company and rectifying, if you will, any distorted images of history. So if it sounds as if you've got a few more rounds of "interviews" lined up once you've gotten your finalist candidate in sight . . . congratulations, you understand where we're going with this topic!

Reference checks are fairly quick, easy, and painless to perform. Compared to the hours that go into interviewing and testing candidates, they therefore have the biggest payback in terms of reward to effort. The questions that follow could themselves be used during the interview. However, they lend themselves better to third-party evaluations than they do to direct communication with a candidate. After all, few if any candidates would admit to having problems accepting constructive criticism, handling interruptions and breaks in routine, or hustling to meet deadlines.

Of course, if you would like to employ some of these questions during an interview, you could phrase them in a behavioral format during your meeting like this: "Tell me, Tom, about the last time some outside influence negatively affected your job performance. . . ." And you'd very well get an honest answer that was indeed grounded in reality. Still, the nature of that issue is better judged by a past supervisor than by the candidate sitting in front of you during an interview.

A special note of interest: If the candidate's past company is out of business or if former supervisors can't be found to pass judgment on the individual's performance, request a recent annual performance appraisal as a condition of hire. It should provide you with fairly objective feedback regarding the individual's strengths, weaknesses, and areas for further training.

Furthermore, beware of past employers who refuse to comment on a candidate's performance. Although one "neutral reference" who only verifies dates of employment and last title held may merely be following his company's official reference policies, too many such employers "taking the fifth" may indicate there were problems with the individual's work. Human nature dictates that past supervisors will help former subordinates whom they liked find other jobs. When "minimum disclosure" patterns begin to occur, on the other hand, it's sometimes because past supervisors would rather say nothing than say something negative about a past employee. If you find that more than one or two former employers refuse to take your calls or strictly quote dates and title, instruct candidates to contact their past employers themselves and bridge the "reference gap" for you.

Finally, remember that this is not a legal treatise aimed at addressing the legal subtleties surrounding confidential and privileged communications between employers regarding candidates' references. Nor is it a forum for discussing employee privacy rights and the potential for accusations of libel, slander, defamation, and negligent hiring. Such issues go beyond the scope of this book and require legal counsel and guidance.

How to Get Employers to Open Up to You During the Reference-Checking Process

The keys to checking references in today's cautious business environment lie in: (1) taking the past supervisor out of the judgmental past and placing him in the evaluative future regarding the candidate's abilities; and (2) removing the perception of potential liability associated with judging a past subordinate's performance, and then replacing it with advice on how to manage this person in order to bring out the best in her abilities. This goal is accomplished in three steps.

Step 1: When opening a conversation with a past supervisor of the employee in question, spread honey on the situation. The appeal of flattery often gets people talking freely:

> "Mary, John Smith said some excellent things about your managerial abilities in terms of giving him clear direction and structure in his day. I was hoping that, reciprocally, you could share some of your insights into his ability to excel in our company. . . ."

Step 2: When beginning the first reference questions, avoid asking generic queries regarding the candidate's job duties, greatest strengths, and areas for improvement. Instead, paint a picture of your corporate culture and its unique pressures so that this supervisor can do some evaluative decision making regarding the individual's "fit factor" into your organization. For example:

> "We're a mortgage banking firm in an intense growth mode. The phones don't stop ringing, the paperwork is endless, and we're considering Mary for a position in our customer service unit that deals with our most demanding customers. Is that an environment in which she would excel?"

Step 3: If the employer is hesitant about sharing performance feedback, replace the notion of "what you tell me will determine whether we hire this person" with an appeal to the employer's managerial expertise:

> "Janet, I won't ask you to address anything you'd rather keep confidential. And I also want you to know that I'm not burdening you with the responsibility of judging this person's past. We're simply at an evaluation stage right now where several candidates are in contention for the job, and we want your advice in terms of how to manage this person most effectively by not having to 'reinvent the wheel' with her. So my questions to you will be in terms of the kind of structure we should provide her in order to give her the most support from day one and make her a success. Are you okay with that?"

Because these questions focus more on future suggestions for supervision and development than traditional queries that pass judgment on past performance, much of the stigma attached to the legal liability issues of sharing reference information will be removed. But what if the employer still won't talk? "Hard-liners" who insist that corporate rules are not to be broken are the ultimate challenge in the reference-checking process. Of course, the impact of one employer's refusal to participate must be kept in perspective: If other employers are giving rave reviews, and this one supervisor refuses to provide feedback under any circumstances, then that silence shouldn't necessarily become a negative swing factor to ultimately disqualify the candidate.

Your last-ditch strategy would be to call an employer back and state:

> "I appreciate your adherence to your corporate reference-checking guidelines. Still, I can't help but assume that no news is bad

news since most employers will give a good reference to help a former worker land a new job if that person was a solid performer. I won't hire this person without your feedback because my assumption at this point is that there were problems. I'll keep what you say totally confidential and off the record, but I'll make her an offer of employment only if you share your insights into her ability to excel in our company."

This appeal to guilt may seem like an unfair stratagem, but there's nothing to lose at this point. Besides, once you've framed your concerns so explicitly, then you could rest assured that further silence on the employer's part represents a tacit agreement with your stated concerns. Finally, close the reference check by asking if the candidate is considered rehirable. A "no comment" response or flat-out "no" should dictate your course of action in evaluating other, more suitable individuals.

Twenty-One

Maximizing Your Recruitment Resources

Selecting outside organizations to help you identify and approach high-performance job candidates can be highly effective if you know how best to utilize their services. Contingency and retained search firms are constantly looking for new clients to add to their rosters, but at what salary level does contingency stop and retainer start? What options do you have for blending the two types of services? What niches have research firms filled vis-à-vis traditional headhunting outfits? And how can outplacement firms help you identify top performers who may currently be in transition through no fault of their own? Let's take each of these issues one at a time and then provide you with resources for further research.

Recruitment Option 1: Contingency Search Firms

Contingency recruiters come in two basic flavors: (1) professional/technical search and (2) administrative support recruitment. You're probably well aware of traditional clerical support agencies that place secretaries, staff accountants, customer services representatives, and the like. Such organizations typically place job candidates earning $40,000 a year and under. Professional/technical agencies, in comparison, usually specialize in individual disciplines like accounting and finance, data processing and information technology, retail, software engineering, and pharmaceutical sales. Such candidates typically earn somewhere between $40,000 and $80,000 a year.

What these firms have in common is that they operate on contingency, meaning that they get paid only if you, the client, hire one of their candidates. The contingency recruitment field is a high-volume, brokerage business that achieves economies of scale by placing candidates with similar skills, knowledge, and abilities into organizations with like needs. That's why they specialize in particular technical disciplines: In searching for candidates with a predetermined profile, agencies develop candidates who simultaneously meet multiple client companies' needs. In short, it's a business set up to prove capitalism right those search firms that are the most successful at meeting clients' demands flourish. Hence, working with contingency recruiters is a win-win situation: You pay only if your needs are met.

Contingency recruiters earn a fee based on a percentage of the candidate's annual salary. The typical formula is 1 percent per thousand of the candidate's first-year earnings, to a maximum of 33 percent. For example, if you're a semiconductor manufacturer looking for a sales engineer who earns $75,000 a year, then your fee to a contingency recruiter who successfully finds someone for you is $24,750, or 33 percent of $75,000. Contingency search firms also offer a safety-net "guarantee period" in case a candidate doesn't work out in the first quarter. Those guarantees usually come in the form of a thirty-day free trial (where the fee you paid is totally refunded) followed by a sixty-day "candidate replacement" period (where the agency replaces the candidate at no additional cost). Although fees and guarantees are sometimes negotiable, this is standard fare in the contingency search industry.

If you need to contact a contingency search firm with professional industry certification, purchase:

The National Directory of Personnel Services ($20.95, 1995 edition)
The National Association of Personnel Services
3133 Mount Vernon Avenue
Alexandria, Virginia 22305
(703) 684-0180

The directory profiles 1,200 member firms in the contingency search and temporary fields of employment. It's divided by job specialty and geographic location to make the job of selecting a placement firm that much easier. And again, companies that have spent the dollars and energy to pass professional exams in order to become better service providers to their clients stand a much better chance of presenting solutions to your staffing needs.

Recruitment Option 2: Retained Search Firms, or "Headhunters"

The retained search business, in comparison, is a much more exclusive game. Retained recruiters typically target candidates making more than

$80,000 for their clients. If, for example, a semiconductor manufacturer is looking for a general manager with an MBA and ten or more years of power electronics experience in the international arena to become part of a $200 million company with 1,200 employees, then a retained recruiter would bid for the business and begin the search.

Of course, there might only be 50 or 100 qualified people in the whole country who meet your exacting criteria. That means that the headhunter would have to spend a great deal of time researching your competition, developing names and profiles of candidates, approaching those candidates with your opportunity, and then qualifying them in terms of their willingness and ability to do the job, fit your company's corporate culture, and potentially relocate.

The whole process is obviously not cost-efficient if done strictly on contingency. So these recruiters work on retainer and typically get paid in three installments: one third of the fee initially to begin the search, one third after thirty days, and one third after sixty days—regardless of whether the search is completed. You are in essence paying for their time and expertise in researching, sourcing, and proactively qualifying candidates who are not currently on the job market. The headhunter acts as an aggressive third party to scout the best people at competing companies and to persuade them to consider a career-advancing move with your firm.

Unlike contingency recruiters who must place a candidate to earn a fee, the retained recruiter gets a fee that is guaranteed up front. Because of that financial arrangement, there is little financial bias to preclude a pure consulting relationship. Consequently, headhunters act like management consultants who attempt to shift the competitive balance of management power in their client company's favor.

The bottom line: Employ a retained search firm for six-figure positions with exacting criteria when your sense of urgency is great and your need for dedicated attention is critical. If you find it difficult to pay a retainer when contingency recruiters will apparently do the same work for free, remember that it wouldn't make sense for contingency recruiters to work a search assignment that's too difficult when they have other, more "fillable" openings to tend to. Retained recruiters, in comparison, will be beholden to you until the assignment is completed because they will already have been paid their fee.

To contact qualified retained search firms in your field, order:

The Directory of Executive Recruiters ($44.95, 1996 edition)
Kennedy Publications
Templeton Road
Fitzwilliam, NH 03447
(800) 531-0007

This well-known "Red Book" is a 990-page paperback with contact information for 3,200 firms in 4,400 locations in North America. It divides both retained and contingency search firms by management function, industry specialty, and geography. It contains the most complete listing of search firms available, and it's an excellent source for identifying search firms' capabilities.

In addition, if you're looking for an overseas search firm for your international recruitment needs, purchase:

The Euro Directory: Executive Search and Selection Firms in Europe
($125, 1st edition 1994)
Published by The Recruiting and Search Report
Publisher: Kenneth J. Cole
P.O. Box 9433
Panama City Beach, FL 32417
(800) 634-4548

The Euro Directory provides profiles and complete contact information for European headhunting organizations from Spain to Poland. It also includes a comprehensive list of major European networking organizations. It's the only work of its kind to aid U.S. employers with the daunting task of selecting search firms overseas, and it does an excellent job of detailing those firms' geographic focuses as well as industry and functional specializations.

Option 3: The Blended "Con-Tainer" Arrangement

One of the newest trends in the contingency search world lies in the creation of a hybrid fee arrangement known affectionately as a "con-tainer" because it attempts to blend the best of both contingency and retained services. This came about after the Great Recession of the early 1990s when contingency recruiters noticed that companies were paying retainers to headhunters for lower-paying positions than usual (in the $50,000 to $60,000 range). Clients apparently liked the dedicated attention afforded them by their retained recruiters, so rather than enlist contingency recruiters once the market picked up, they simply maintained the relationships established with their headhunters—even for lower-paying positions.

Well, if contingency recruiters handled $40,000 to $80,000 searches (as always), and headhunters now began handling similar-paying searches on retainer, then why not, reasoned the contingency folks, offer clients the option of paying partial retainers? This way the client gets that dedicated attention like retained firms offer, but the company is not obligated to pay the entire fee unless the assignment is filled. (Ah, isn't capitalism great?!)

To further sweeten the deal, contingency recruiters often make the aggregate "con-tainer" payment cheaper than the traditional contingency arrangement. Here's how it works: Let's go back to our $75,000 semiconductor sales engineer candidate again.

Traditional Contingency Fee Arrangement

At 33 percent contingency, the fee equals $24,750:

$75,000 base salary
×   33 percent fee arrangement
$24,750 fee for hire

Sample "Con-tainer" Fee Arrangement

$75,000 base salary
×   18 percent negotiated fee arrangement (not 33 percent)
$13,500
+ $5,000 nonrefundable fee retained up front
$18,500 fee for hire

That's $6,250 less than a strict contingency arrangement!

Why would contingency search firms offer that? First, to win the business away from retained search firms. And second, to keep you working with them exclusively. (After all, you're not going to list that search with other contingency recruiters if you've already invested $5000 of your money with one firm, right?) It's a viable attempt on the contingency recruiter's part to offer a creative alternative to the traditional search arrangement. Put a pencil to paper and see whether this option could save you valuable recruitment dollars as well!

Option 4: Research Firms

As another alternative to traditional contingency or retained recruitment, research firms package their services into hourly paid increments. For example, you might enlist a research firm only to research and identify prospective candidates. The fee would then be based on the number of hours necessary to generate the candidate list. You, the client, could also pay extra for the research firm to approach, qualify, interview, and reference-check those candidates.

In essence, the firm "unbundles" the search process into its component parts, thereby providing you with significant cost control measures by allowing you to bring in house parts of an activity that formerly had to be totally outsourced. As such, research organizations are a very logical and necessary component in today's environment of cost reductions and expense controls.

To locate a listing of research firms that handle "unbundled search," order:

The Executive Search Research Directory ($125, 7th edition, 1994)
Published by The Recruiting and Search Report
Publisher: Kenneth J. Cole
P.O. Box 9433
Panama City Beach, FL 32417
(800) 634-4548

The directory provides critical information regarding researchers' areas of concentration, specialties, and unusual expertise. It does an excellent job of helping you select firms to conduct the most important initial segment of any search assignment: the research.

Option 5: Outplacement Firms' Job Development Departments

Outplacement firms are paid by companies that are downsizing to assist displaced workers in finding jobs. When companies demonstrate concern for hastened reemployment of laid-off workers, they foster a sense that people are well taken care of, and that automatically minimizes the traumatic impact on remaining employees. As far as the company is concerned, the cost of outplacement (typically 15 percent of the displaced worker's base salary) is far outweighed by the altruistic and practical benefits that allow it to continue its business operations without undue interruption.

It is in the outplacement firm's best interests to get their candidates placed as quickly as possible. That's because it costs outplacement firms lots of money to provide services for displaced executives, like telephone and fax access, word processing support for cover letters and resumes, secretarial support, and the like. It's estimated that if a candidate remains on the outplacement firm's books for more than six months, the outplacement firm loses money on that transaction. (That up-front 15 percent fee gets more than consumed once the individual has used up more than six months of services).

Therefore, outplacement firms employ job developers to help their candidates find work. Those job developers are constantly soliciting job openings from other companies and encouraging their candidates to seize the opportunities available. Remember that because the outplacement firm is paid by the candidate's old company, not by you (the potential new employer), this free supply of talent could significantly reduce your cost per hire. If you're unsure of this source because you feel that the candidates from outplacement firms are the ones who "couldn't make the cut," don't be! Companies have downsized entire divisions in this era of mergers, acquisitions, and divestitures, and many of the candidates now in outplacement's care were being placed by retained search firms five years ago. Outplacement firms are an incredible source of free, highly qualified candidates, and it would be an absolute mistake not to list your openings with them.

Following are the three largest outplacement firms in the nation. Their job banks are national, so listing a job opening will give you vast exposure. Also, if you want to keep the identity of your company confidential or if you want only those resumés that meet certain criteria, the job developers will do all that and more for you. Take advantage of this free and effective service immediately by faxing, mailing, or e-mailing your job openings to the following job banks:

Right Associates
Corporate Headquarters
1818 Market Street, 33rd Floor
Philadelphia, PA 19103-3614
(800) 237-4448
Job Bank Fax: (215) 988-0081

Drake Beam Morin
Corporate Headquarters
100 Park Avenue, 4th Floor
New York, NY 10017
(212) 692-7700
Job Bank Fax: (212) 808-0253

Lee Hecht Harrison
Corporate Headquarters
200 Park Avenue, 26th Floor
New York, NY 10166
(212) 557-0009
"Lead Link" Job Bank Fax : (212) 557-9807
World Wide Web address for job listings:
   http://www.careerlhh.com

Interviewer's Checklist:
The 96 Questions

1. Tell me about your greatest strength. What's the greatest asset you'll bring to our company?
2. What's your greatest weakness?
3. What was your favorite position, and what role did your boss play in making it so unique?
4. What was your least favorite position? What role did your boss play in your career at that point?
5. Where do you see yourself in five years?
6. What makes you stand out among your peers?
7. What have you done on your present/last position to increase your organization's top-line revenues?
8. What have you done to reduce your department's operational costs or to save time?
9. What has been your most creative achievement at work?
10. What would your current supervisors say makes you most valuable to them?
11. What are the broad responsibilities of a [*job title*]?
12. What aspects of your job do you consider most crucial?
13. How many hours a week do you find it necessary to work in order to get your job done?
14. How does your position relate to the overall goals of your department or company?
15. What area of your skills do you need to improve upon in the next year?
16. How many employees were laid off simultaneously?
17. How many people survived the cut?
18. How many waves of layoffs did you survive before you were let go yourself?

19. What does growth mean to you?
20. What will you do differently at your present company if you don't get this position?
21. Describe how you've progressed through the ranks and landed in your current position at ABC Company.
22. How have you added value to your job over time?
23. How have you had to reinvent or redefine your job to meet your company's changing needs? What proactive steps did you have to take to increase the output of your position?
24. Distinguish between your vertical progression through the ranks at your last/present company and your lateral assumption of broader responsibilities.
25. What would be your next logical move in progression at your present company?
26. What kind of mentoring and training style do you have? Do you naturally delegate responsibilities, or do you expect your direct reports to come to you for added responsibilities?
27. Every company has its own quirks—its "dysfunctionality quotient," so to speak. How dysfunctional was your last company, and how much tolerance do you have for dealing with a company's shortcomings and inconsistencies?
28. How would you describe the amount of structure, direction, and feedback that you need to excel?
29. In terms of managing your staff, do you "expect" more than you "inspect," or vice versa?
30. How do you approach your work from the standpoint of balancing your career with your personal life?
31. Paint a picture of the corporate culture you'll create if we hire you. Do you operate under a more centralized and paternalistic agenda with power centralized in the hands of a few, or do you constantly push responsibility and accountability down the line?
32. Why did you choose your [*college/major*]?
33. How does your degree prepare you (a) for a career in [*industry*] or (b) to excel as a [*job title*]?
34. What qualifications do you have beyond academics that qualify you to make a successful transition into business?
35. Do you think your grades are a good indicator of your ability to succeed in business?
36. What other types of positions and companies are you considering right now?
37. How would you grade your ability to predict needs before they arise?

In other words, how would you evaluate your intuition, timeliness, and proactive business style?

38. Do you consider your technical abilities basic, intermediate, or advanced? What types of projects did you complete with each software program?

39. In what areas do you typically have the least amount of patience at work?

40. How would you grade your ability to communicate with upper-level management, customers, and peers?

41. What pace do you typically work at?

42. How do you competitively rank among other account executives in terms of your production?

43. What are the two most common objections you face, and how do you deal with them?

44. Role-play with me, if you will, presenting yourself to me over the phone as if you were a headhunter. Convince me that this "product" you're selling is worth my time.

45. How do you define your closing style?

46. All salespeople need to find an equilibrium between (a) high-volume production numbers and (b) quality. Which philosophy drives your sales style more?

47. Tell me about the last time you failed to meet quota. How many times did that happen over the past year, and what plan of action did you take to get back on track?

48. With no undue flattery, if you will, grade me on how well I'm conducting this interview: What can you tell me about my sales and management style on the basis of the questions I'm asking you?

49. How important is the base salary component to you? Would you prefer a straight commission if it offered you the potential for an additional 35 percent in aggregate earnings over the base salary?

50. Tell me about your quality ratios: How many prospects do you typically see before closing a sale?

51. How much does production vary from desk to desk in your office?

52. Give me an example of your ability to facilitate progressive change within your organization.

53. Tell me about the last time you inherited a problem unit—one suffering from poor productivity or low morale. What was the scope of the project, and how were your direct reports affected?

54. Did you create a culture of open information sharing and increased accountability by giving responsibility to your subordinates, or did you focus more on establishing their parameters and controlling the decision-making process?

55. How do you typically stay in the information loop and monitor your staff's performance?
56. How do you typically confront subordinates when results are unacceptable?
57. Tell me about the your last performance appraisal. In which area were you most disappointed?
58. In hindsight, how could you have improved your performance at your last position?
59. Where do you disagree with your boss most often? How did you handle the last time she was wrong and you were right?
60. How would your supervisor grade your ability to cope with last-minute change without breaking stride?
61. Why do you want to work here?
62. What do you know about our company?
63. Tell me about your understanding of the job you're applying for.
64. What can you do for us if we hire you, and when should we expect to see concrete results?
65. How structured an environment would you say this individual needs to reach her maximum potential?
66. Does this individual typically adhere strictly to job duties, or does he assume responsibilities beyond the basic, written job description?
67. Please comment on this person's ability to accept constructive criticism.
68. How much do outside influences play a role in her job performance?
69. Would you consider this individual more of a task-oriented or project-oriented worker?
70. How does he handle interruptions, breaks in routine, and last-minute changes?
71. How would you grade her commitment to project completion?
72. How would you grade this candidate's capacity for analytical thinking and problem solving?
73. Does this individual need close supervision to excel, or does she take more of an autonomous, independent approach to her work?
74. How global a perspective does he have? Do you see him eventually making the transition from a tactical and operational career path to the strategic level necessary for a career in senior management?
75. How would you grade this candidate's listening skills?
76. How effective is the candidate at delivering bad news? Will he typically assume responsibility for things gone wrong?
77. Please grade the individual's capacity for initiative and taking action. Does she have a tendency to get bogged down in "analysis paralysis"?

78. Is this candidate's management style more autocratic and paternalistic or is it geared toward a more participative and consensus-building approach?
79. In terms of this individual's energy level, how would you grade his capacity for hustle?
80. How does this individual approach taking action without getting prior approval?
81. Is it this person's natural inclination to report to someone else for sign-off, or does she operate better with independent responsibility and authority?
82. After so many years in the business, is this candidate still on a career track for which she can sustain enthusiasm?
83. How effective is this person at orchestrating a corporate ensemble of functional areas?
84. Please address the candidate's ability to cope with the significant pressures associated with senior management.
85. Does this person ever delay the inevitable in terms of disciplining or dismissing employees?
86. Is this individual inclined to maintain smooth and amicable relations at all costs, or is she more likely to show her teeth when faced with adversity?
87. Does the candidate stay open to all sides of an argument before reaching a decision, or does he get personally involved in conflicts?
88. Tell me again why you feel the position you're applying for meets your career needs or why working for our company is so important for you.
89. On a scale of 1 to 10 (10 being you're really excited about accepting our offer, 1 being there's no interest), where do you stand?
90. What would have to change at your present position for you to continue working there?
91. Tell me about the counteroffer they'll make you once you give notice. If you gave notice to your boss right now, what would he say to keep you?
92. What's changed since the last time we spoke?
93. If you had to choose among three factors—(1) the company, (2) the position you're applying for, or (3) the people you'd be working with—which would you say plays the most significant role in your decision to accept our offer?
94. If we were to make you an offer, tell me ideally when you'd like to start. How much notice would you need to give your present employer?

95. Share with me what final questions I can answer for you to help you come to an informed career decision.
96. At what dollar level would you accept our job offer, and at what dollar level would you reject it?

Index